Q

Queer Space

Architecture and Same-Sex Desire

AARON BETSKY

WILLIAM MORROW AND COMPANY, INC. NEW YORK

Other Books by Aaron Betsky

Building Sex

Violated Perfection: Architecture
and the Fragmentation of the Modern

James Gamble Rogers and the Architecture of Pragmatism

Library of Congress Cataloging-in-Publication Data

Betsky, Aaron.
    Queer space : architecture and same-sex desire / by Aaron Betsky.
        p.   cm.
    Includes bibliographical references and index.
    ISBN 0-688-14301-6
    1. Homosexuality and architecture.   I. Title.
NA2543.H65B48 1997
720 ' .8664—DC20   96-15992 CIP

Printed in the United States of America

First Edition

1   2   3   4   5   6   7   8   9   10

BOOK DESIGN BY TENAZAS DESIGN SAN FRANCISCO

Acknowledgments

This project started as a class I taught at the Southern California Institute of

Architecture in Los Angeles during the spring of 1994.

I am extremely grateful to all the students who participated
in this seminar, found invaluable resources for me,
and helped me to articulate many of the ideas in this book.
Kevin McMahon, who is the librarian at this school, has served
as my conscience and my adviser as I was formulating this
book. His comments were succinct, to the point, and revealing.
In addition, I received advice and valuable research resources
from Jonathan Boorstein, James Benjamin, David Dunlap,
and Richard Snyder. Jim Grimes and Samuel Yates
were extremely helpful research assistants. Jaime Rua helped
edit and shape the final manuscript. Finally, I could not have
completed this book without the love and support of
Peter Christian Haberkorn.

Queer Space

Architecture and Same-Sex Desire

Contents

Some Q*ueer Constructs*

Introduction

I was dreamin when I wrote this

So sue me if I go too fast

But life is just a party

And parties weren't meant to last

War is all around us, my mind says prepare to fight

So if I gotta die I'm gonna listen to

My body tonight cuz they say

2000 zero zero party over oops out of time[1]

I was still an architecture student learning the
correct orders and order of things when I would
come down to New York late at night and walk
the streets of Midtown, broad and deserted at
night, until I came to the small crowd gathered
around the door of Studio 54. A doorman,
often clad in an oversized parka, stood on a raised stoop, singling out those
who were, for some reason of fashion or urban mix, worthy.

Passing through the barricades, you would enter into a long hallway, the
music and lights already echoing through the space. Then you would erupt into a
domed vastness, its edges unknowable, packed with people. Lasers and light beams
rotated through this darkness, sectioning off slices of space into defined layers, spots,
and even rooms. Mirrors would come down off the ceiling, so that you could dance
with yourself instead of others. After a later renovation, a bank of red and blue neon
lights would create a flat ceiling, a gabled roof, walls, or rotating saucers around the

dancers. As the crowds grew, the invisible wizards up in the booth would use the lights, music, and props to press them ever closer together, pushing and pulling at the space until the whole room was filled to capacity and the bare brick wall that backed up what used to be the stage emerged, complete with the original stage lighting.

Then suddenly everything would go black, and an ethereal silence would descend. Bodies would emerge as the crowd melted away. Nearly nude males would wrap themselves up in shadows, adoring themselves in motion. Upstairs, on the balcony, voyeurs would watch, or would engage in their own, more intimate dances, discovering their bodies in others. "What are we celebrating?" a friend asked as we watched a particular intense evening of choreographed spaces unfold below us from that vantage point. "It's the end of the world, that's what," answered another.

"This is the Versailles of the twentieth century," said the same friend that evening. I tend to agree. This was the *Gesamtkunstwerk* that New York produced in the 1980s, when all the money and cultural talent of the world crowded into the small island. It translated wealth into a dense experience, structured by a variety of different technologies. It was a spectacle that brought to life a vision of a liberated, joyous, and sensual existence that was at the same time no more than a reflection of a morally bankrupt, greedy elite. Inside Studio 54, a new world was born, but it would have no issue, it would make no difference, it would save nothing. It was pure act. Like Versailles, it was a lavish place, a place that made you feel powerful and important. It relied on ritual, role-playing, and operatic exaggeration. It made you feel as if you were building a brave new world as the old world and its facts dissolved. It did so in a way that never took itself seriously. This was, after all, just a dance club.

It was the most powerful architecture I knew.

The spaces that appeared and disappeared there every night were so much more clearly focused, so much more direct. Exactly because they did not stick around long enough to accrue meanings, memories, or emotions, they confronted you much more clearly as nothing but pure space, activated only by your body. Instead of walls, floors, and ceilings, here was a space that appeared and disappeared continually. Instead of places of privacy, where design was unwanted, and public spaces where architecture had to appear in a correct guise, here was a place where the most intimate acts, whether real or acted out in dance, occurred in full view through a structure of lights, sounds, and arrangements that made it all seem natural. Instead of references to buildings or paintings, instead of a grammar of ornament and a syntax of facades, here was only rhythm and light.

Looking back on it, this was queer space. In this book, I will try to describe what I mean by that phrase. It is a kind of space that I find liberating, and that I think might help us avoid some of the imprisoning characteristics of the modern city. It is a useless, amoral, and sensual space that lives only in and for experience. It is a space of spectacle, consumption, dance, and obscenity. It is a misuse or deformation of a place, an appropriation of the buildings and codes of the city for perverse purposes. It is a space in between the body and technology, a space of pure artifice.

All of these grand terms and definitions go back to a particular cultural condition: that experienced by homosexual men in the Western world in the twentieth century. It is my contention that because of the particular place that this group of people occupied at that time, they produced spaces with characteristics we might call queer. These queer spaces infected and inflected our built environment, pointing the way toward an opening, a liberating possibility. Almost as soon as they were stated, they disappeared into that culture as their very power became useful for advertising, lifestyles, and the occupation of real estate.

I will not claim that it was only homosexual men who created these environments, or that one has to be homosexual and male to recognize them. I will only argue that queer men queered space by using techniques borrowed from many other sources. Straight men, straight and queer women, and people whose genders and preferences we cannot know also created such spaces.[2] Queer culture appropriated such efforts and used them to good effect. Then popular culture used them to even better and more productive ends.

In my last book, *Building Sex*,[3] I argued that men in the Western world have created architecture, and women have been forced to live in its often confining structures. In return, women have used their interiors to create often beautiful, sensual, comfortable, and practical environments, divorced as they have been from overt "meanings." To a large extent this is still true, but changes in technology and in the roles men and women play have opened up some new places. Because they were defined as "the third sex," queer men and, to a lesser degree, queer women have been the first—but I hope not the last—to explore these possibilities.

The traditions that exploded out into Studio 54 all come out of the fringes or odd corners of our culture. They include stagecraft, the creation of artificial, inward-turned worlds for same-sex groups, the communal evocation of Bohemian worlds of decadence, the urge to collect objects and then assemble them into highly personal maps or mirrors of an unseen or unpresentable self, the use of the public scene for obscene purposes, a conscious living in ruins and forgotten places in order to create a new community, a bacchanalian celebration of community through the body, a choreographic of spaces and experiences, and the use of technology as a conscious insertion into or imposition on the body.

What I am talking about, in other words, is how queer men put on a show. It was a show that presented them first of all to themselves, validating their existence in a real place, and then to others who shared their tastes, so that they might recognize each other, and, finally and defiantly, to the world. It was, in other words, an expressive and condensed working through of what architecture always does: it allows us to place ourselves in the world, define ourselves in relation to others, and create another, artificial world that replaces the one we have remade. The cabaret, the extravagant opera set, the interior "designed for seduction," as one observer put it,[4] the restaurant activated by the flaneur—all of these have a seriously outrageous message: we make and are made by our own spaces.

Why is it that queer men managed to stage, in an almost didactic way, a pageant of the history of architecture? How is that they managed to create some of the most articulated, focused, and self-consciously *other* spaces in Western culture? It is my contention that they did this because they had to make conscious the particular situation of the middle class. I do not mean this to be a social tract, but I think that we must not forget that we are talking about the freedom that a certain relatively small group of people had to use the enormous resources reserved for the well-off in our society. They employed them to make places, and did so, because of the restrictions put on that use, more creatively than most.

I am therefore not talking here in general about same-sex desires and how they might lead to the creation of a certain social persona. I am not so much interested in what makes someone gay, queer, or homosexual—

all terms that define different shadings of what one or society makes out of one's desires—as I am in how a distinct culture emerged around those desires. Though it is true that there have been other subcultures, networks, and defined social groups throughout history that have defined themselves through same-sex desires, I am interested specifically in the roots, development, flowering, and, what is most important, effect of a particular culture that I will, almost arbitrarily, define as queer.[5]

Queerness, I would argue, emerged with the middle class in the middle of the nineteenth century. Its roots go back, as I will show, to the first foundations of a class of merchants, tradespeople, and clerks who were neither owners nor workers, but the makers of an in-between space. This was a space that was urban, removing itself both from the country and the isolated palaces of the rich. It was defined by technology, allowing this same class to abstract the riches of the earth into the finished and consumable goods through which they then defined themselves. It was in the shadows of the first stock exchanges, along the trading routes of an emerging public infrastructure, and through the rationalization of language and behavior that queerness as we know it today first emerged. This was no longer the same-sex love of older men for younger partners, or of owners for their slaves. This was not even the sensual friendship among equals of rarefied tastes. This was the love of sex and companionship with members of one's sex, negotiated through a careful set of rules, gestures, and conventions.

As many observers, starting with Karl Marx and Friedrich Engels, have pointed out, this middle class justified its very existence as both individuals and a class through the creation of a culture that glorified exactly individuality and the creation of a man-made world. It evaluated itself, and created value, out of thin air, by its own industry or artifice. It was fundamentally disconnected from the production and reproduction of material reality.[6]

Architecture was a central part of this activity. It gave us models of a perfectly planned world in which efficiency, organization, and usefulness would reign supreme, creating a perfectly proportioned and moral environment. Only in and through these spaces could the middle class validate itself. The city and the suburb, the domestic environment and the place of work, the promenade and the bar— these were the spaces that made the lives of the middle class.[7]

Figure I.2
Drawing Room,
Schroeder
Residence,
New York,
1903

A particular segment of the middle class had to define itself self-consciously. The middle class invented certain institutions that it used to order its new space, and that became reflected in buildings. These included the nuclear family (the single-family house and the suburb), the regimented and defined body (the gymnasium and the boys' school, but also prisons), and the notion of a correct way of public behavior through which one might present oneself (public squares and boulevards). None of these worked too well for queer men. They did not have families at the cores of their life, the disciplining of the body turned into its reverse, i.e., the satisfaction of desire, and public space was where the queer man had to hide his desire. They were the other side, or ob-scene, of the middle class scene.

There were other spaces.

If the middle class created a new space cordoning off an artificial zone of security within a world it continued to change all around itself, then the closet was the ultimate interior. It was the ultimate condensation of such a zone.[8] It was the place at the heart of the home, where a queer man could confront his own body in secrecy. Mirroring one's self in an artificial appearance, or "passing" as straight, was the ultimate mode of correct behavior, and the network of queers that traced the social and economic relations of the middle class became a sort of "family" (as some queers still call each other). Certain places became the nuclei for the most carefully choreographed spaces of appearance, where public space and appearance melded together to create a truly modern invention: the homosexual, prowling, like a perverted flaneur, the public rest rooms (end point of the vast sanitary systems that made the city safe from nature), hiding in the mirrored world of the bar, or building up a fantastical world by gathering objects from all times and places.[9]

Figure I.3
Anonymous,
Detail of
Les Nymphes du Palais Royal,
1815

Certain types emerged who highlighted both middle-class and homosexual values. Collectors, such as William Beckford, created whole fantasy interior landscapes from which they rarely emerged. The home as a collection of artifacts that defined the individual by serving as an objective map of his passions, by evoking other worlds than the one in which he was imprisoned, and by mirroring him in objects became a queer version of the self-enclosed world of the family.

Out in the city, flaneurs such as Baudelaire and Oscar Wilde expressed the very delight in an escape from nature. They used the city as their playground, the bars as their meeting places, and the population as objects of use. They defined themselves by creating a collective culture (closely associated with aestheticism and the Arts and Crafts movement), by delighting in the exoticism of other classes (Wilde loved both working-class and aristocratic, but not middle-class, men), and by exploring the furthest reaches of the new urban environment. They found within it possibilities that planners had never considered. The city could be reformed and cruised.

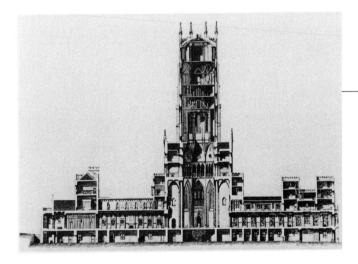

Figure I.4
James Wyatt,
Fonthill Abbey,
Wiltshire,
1812
(longitudinal
section)

Others delighted in the discipline of technology, whether expressed in the violence of war or bondage or in the emptying of all space that left nothing but the abstract grid of pure modernism. Thus the naked, solipsistic body could become part of the machine. Though this desire may have failed, the ritual is repeated by gays today in the endless rounds at the gym.

Yet others played with the continual ironic deformation of types, highlighting their very constructed nature by lampooning them, changing their uses, or melting them into oceanic currents. Such was the work of architects and designers such as Louis Sullivan, Ralph Adams Cram, Cecil Beaton, and Charles de Beistegui. These designers always sought the most elaborated version of a historical style like neo-Gothicism or classicism, where it folded in on itself to the point of dissolving. They wove those forms together into the filigree decorations of churches or the waves of iron that spilled over the facades of Chicago's department stores. They made fun of correct orders, revealing the thinness of walls and the insubstantiality of columns. To them, the world was a stage set. The realization that nothing in the middle-class world was real, that it was all appearances, led naturally to the delight in stage sets, mirrors, and thin, tentlike encampments in the rational grids of the city.

Certain places appeared: the club, the salon, and the momentary spaces of the "tearoom" or public rest room turned into orgy spaces. The bathhouse and other realms of sensuality offered respite from the world, and thus became escape valves for society as a whole. In such isolated places, the very notion of creating a new world, with its own appearances and modes of appearance, could be forged. Yet all such ideals could also be forgotten, as the middle-class man was brought back to the seemingly elemental fact of his body, thus escaping the constrictions of appearance. Queer spaces melded utopian and corporeal escape, a movement inward with a movement outward. The city was rewritten by men cruising and refusing to accept its strictures.

Figure I.5
Paul Cadmus,
Vacationers,
1944

Inside the domestic environment itself, queer women were sloughing off the bonds of conventions. They turned the layers of accumulated self-definition into the all-white world of Elsie de Wolfe, where machinery and decoration fed on each other to create a sensible and sensual setting for women only. Julia Morgan, building on a network of women's organizations, opened up the exotic world of California to the sun, the water, and the land, creating realistic fantasies that opposed the pure escapism of some of her contemporaries with a sense of deliberate normalcy.

In all of these ways, queers queered the city.

They made it their own, they opened it up on the margins, they performed it. They were always a minority, but because they were at the very heart of the middle-class project to create an artificial world, their contributions to that culture were immense. They made the spaces that appeared in the movies and the magazines, and designed the clothes in which men and women alike appeared. They made some of the strongest designs on and of the modern world.

In the late twentieth century, they queered the rigid statements of modernism, which sought to give the most condensed and abstracted statement of the man-made world, into the more sensual, ambivalent, and livable forms of postmodernism. They made the city inhabitable again, leading the charge of gentrification that finally liberated the city from the working class. Confronted by their own mortality, they brought the body back into play, making us aware of the machinery, morals, myths, limits, and potentials of a body that could be built, wasted, and explored.

This is what queer men contributed to the modern world. It is a project that is not yet over, and the queer experience continues to be one of the creation of a thoroughly modern world for one's self. Queers continue to queer our cities, our suburbs, and now our exurbs because they must, as they continue to redefine who we are as individuals, as bodies, as part of a society. They continue to restage the promise that we can make ourselves by making a place for ourselves. They are queer moderns.

At the same time, queers are disappearing. We are all becoming part of a consumer society in which there is a premium on interchangeable, malleable data, icons, and symbols. As operators of symbolic logic, we are increasingly post-middle-class, post-individual, post-body. There is no time or place for presentation, for family, for celebration, or for fear. There is only room for plugging in and jacking in, interacting and play-acting. Queer spaces are disappearing, as are most spaces of experience. Out in the suburbs, queers are starting families that are no stranger than those of the single-parent, oft-divorced, and always-moving standard unit. They are networking on the Internet and through twelve-step programs that are indistinguishable from those of their heterosexual peers. The spaces of cruising, though still present, have less of a sense of concentrated activity. Like the edge cities that are taking over our urban life, the life of queer men and women is dissolving into pieces and parts of an endlessly developing sameness.

If to be queer is to be other, uncertain, in between,

self-constructed, free within the confines of power, aware of your body and afraid of its limits, conscious of your own construction and amused by its pretensions, can there be a queer space still? Is it a space beyond "the third sex"? Can there be an opening that is queer toward what cannot be known? In many ways, this is a rhetorical (and queer) question. To refuse to accept one's condition, to build in the full knowledge that one will never finish and never live in peace, is human. It is also, as I hope this book will be, a tantalizing speculation.

Figure I.6
John Anthony,
Steambath,
1988

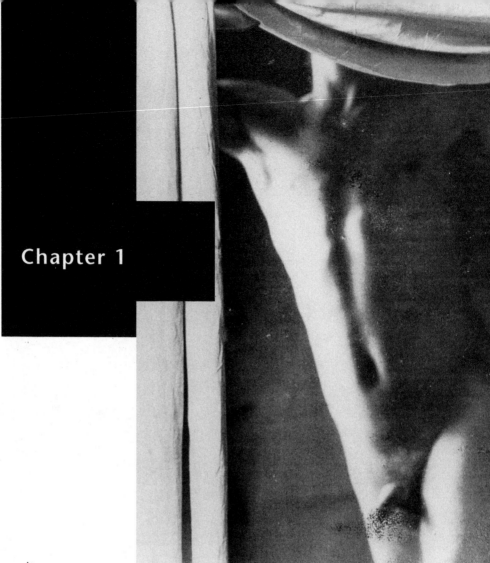

Chapter 1

1

The grammar of the gay city

borrows metaphors from

the nineteenth-century house.

"Coming out of the closet"

is predicated upon family laundry,

dirty linen, skeletons.[1]

Closet Cases and Mirror Worlds

Queers are supposed to be in the closet.
You might say that queer space is born in the closet. What is the closet?
It is the ultimate interior, the place where interiority starts. It is a dark space
at the heart of the home. It is not a place where you live, but where you
store the clothes in which you appear. It contains the building blocks for
your social constructions, such as your clothes. The closet also contains the

disused pieces of your past. It is a place to hide, to create worlds for yourself out of the past and for the future in a secure environment. If the hearth is the heart of the home, where the family gathers to affirm itself as a unit in the glow of the fire, the closet contains both the secret recesses of the soul and the masks you wear. Being in the closet means that you surround yourself with the emblems of your past and with the clothes you can wear, while covering yourself in darkness.[2]

The closet is the opposite of the ordered place of appearance, but also its beginning point. It is a dark and musty place where past and future mingle and could become interchanged. It is where you can define yourself, constructing an identity out of what you have collected, in a space that is free and boundless exactly because it hides in the dark recesses. It is a constructed version of the womb that contains not biological but socially produced building blocks for the person you become in the real world. It is also a place where you return to your body—especially in the "water closet" or toilet.

If queer space starts in the closet,
it forms itself in the mirror.

The mirror is where you appear to yourself, primping and posing, examining and admiring yourself. In the mirror, you and your world, including your body, your clothes, and the objects you have collected around yourself, come back to you in an ordered fashion. Mirror space is an alternate world that is unreal. Everything in it is only a reflection, and yet appears as it really is, only reversed. Mirror space is free and open, shifting and ephemeral, and yet constrained by its lack of reality. The mirror is good for nothing else than appearing: as soon as you look away from it, it ceases to function. You can't live in the mirror.[3]

The goal of queer space is orgasm. There is a space of orgasm. It is the space in which your body dissolves into the world and your senses smooth all reality into continuous waves of pleasure. It only lasts for a moment, but during that moment you give yourself over to pure pleasure made flesh. Orgasmic space leaves you vulnerable and happy in that vulnerability, because you are at the center of your experiences. It is an unreal space with no endurance, and yet is very real.

Figure 1.2
Jean Cocteau,
Orphée:
Jean Marais
with Mirror,
1950

Queer space is built up out of these three elements. Out of the recesses of the self it constructs a mirror in which you appear, then dissolves into orgasm. What I am calling queer space is that which appropriates certain aspects of the material world in which we all live, composes them into an unreal or artificial space, and uses this counterconstruction to create the freespace of orgasm that dissolves the material world.

By its very nature, queer space is something that is not built, only implied, and usually invisible. Queer space does not confidently establish a clear, ordered space for itself. It does not partake in the competition for building the largest house, the tallest tower, or the straightest street. It does not try to make the richest facade, capture the corner office with its doubled views, or stake out an empty space that is your own and not someone else's. It is altogether more ambivalent, open, leaky, self-critical or ironic, and ephemeral. Queer space often doesn't look like an order you can recognize, and when it does, it seems like an ironic or rhetorical twist on such an order.

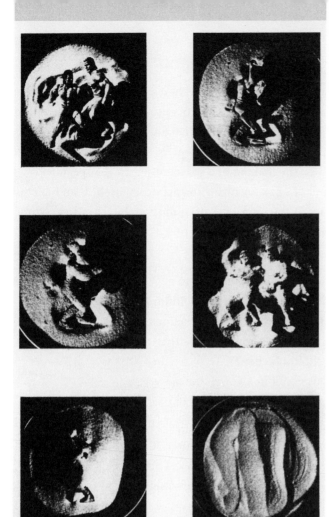

Figure 1.3
Peter Christian
Haberkorn,
*Action Figure
Orgasm,*
1996

It turns out that this is not necessarily just because same-sex love has always been illegal or taboo and therefore has had to hide itself. It has, in fact, been honored or merely assumed in most civilizations. It has never been, however, part of the way in which a society regulated itself. Because it separates itself off from reproduction, it does not have a part in the establishment of the most basic territory of all, that which perpetuates the self through offspring. Queer space is not about building homes, which are some of the simplest building blocks of our physical environment. That does not mean that queers do not or did not live in houses, but the notion of a retreat toward an incubator of values that perpetuate themselves in children has never been a central part of the queer experience.

Because it implies sex among equals, surrender to someone older without clear benefit other than the satisfaction of desire, or the domination of someone for the same reason, it does not represent a productive purpose. Thus queer space has rarely been about corner offices, assembly lines, or bureaucratic palaces. Because same-sex love often presents itself in drag, with one partner playing the part society has assigned to the other sex (though such roles might be arbitrary), it has a hard time putting on a simple, conventional facade.

Same-sex love always comes back to the body, exactly because that is what society has often outlawed. Because same-sex love mirrors the body, it has a hard time accepting an abstract, rational, and alien order. What remains hidden must become revealed, or at least available, through the structure of queer space. The purpose of queer space is again ultimately sex: the making of a space either for that peculiar definition of the self as an engine of sexuality or for the act of sex itself. If architecture sublimates, queer space expresses. If the interiors within most architectural structures accommodate, queer space seduces.

Architecture has in the Western world been a window to a more perfect world. People just build; architects propose a better solution, a rational structure that will make your life better. It proposes abstractions independent of daily life. Those structures turn out, of course, to be the ideas of whoever is in power about how life should be better. They are the spatial version of a pie in the sky that keeps us going in a search for more space for our home, that corner office, an escape into the suburbs, or a grander surrounding.

It is a little different in queer space. Same-sex love is, after all, about the love of the same, a kind of idealized (or perverted, if you will) mirroring of the self in another. The essence of queer love is that it loves itself in another form, or loves another form that it wishes were itself. Its will to power is turned back on itself.

This does not mean that queer space is merely a voluptuous blanket or a gilded mirror. *When you look in a mirror, you always see yourself reversed,* and same-sex love never finds its true self in the other with which it has (or wants to have) sex. Queer space is therefore shot through with tensions, fissures, and contradictions. Sometimes it expresses itself as a rhetorical question (as in sadomasochism), begging the question rather than posing the solution. At that point, it seeks to incorporate, in the literal sense of that word, the orders imposed on it into the body, so that they can dissolve in a sensation of pain closely allied to that of orgasm.[4]

At other times, queer space displaces the body into materials, decoration, and the manipulation of sensual forms. At its most romantic, queer space wants to dissolve the structures and strictures of society and obliterate the space between the self and the other, engaging in sex as part of a voluptuous extension of the body into an oceanic world. This is perhaps the essence of queer space. If we live in physical orders (buildings) society has imposed on us, queer space finds in the closet or the dark alley places where it can construct an artificial architecture of the self. Having appropriated the imposed orders of society, it then poses an alternative—mirror space—that might let all of reality and the self dissolve into something that is pure sensation or bodily experience.

2

There are distinct mechanisms queers use to construct such a space. First, queer space finds its origin in the closet, the place of hiding and constructing one's own identity. It creates itself in darkness, in the obscene, in the hidden. It is a secret condensation of the orders of the home. Rather than allowing you to live in the fiction of established structures, which of course depend on a consent to live together, on economic development, and on institutionalized social practices, it proposes a world of fantasy that is directly related to the body and has no definite space. This is a harrowing, spooky space, but also one that is free from outside constraints.

Second, it uses mirrors. If conventional architecture is more like a window into a perfect world, a fragment of a utopian world that we build every time we construct something new, then queer space just brings us back to ourselves. If queer space establishes itself at all, it surrounds us in a space that is often as invisible or as thin as the surface of a mirror. Mirror space is a strangely haunting space, one where the world comes back to us in a reversed manner. Everything is still there, in place but out of place. As a result, mirror space both affirms and confuses or destabilizes us.[5]

The actions that come out of these spaces of mirror and closet, the methods by which queer space is actually constructed, encompass a choreography of gestures. Gesture is that which comes between the word and the body, between the order of communication that creates an artificial environment and the reality of lived experience.[6] Gesture exaggerates the body, extending it into space, breaking through the mute boundaries of the skin to create a deformed image of the self in a social relationship. Gesture allows for freedom, because it can form an unspoken code that escapes notice and thus control.[7] Gesture is ephemeral, lasting only as long as the act, and is nothing but the act itself: it leaves little residue.

In our society, we have conventionalized and institutionalized gesture in acting, whether formally (onstage) or in the street. Queers are masters of the hidden gesture, the theatrical walk, the creation of close physical connections through the most fleeting motions of the body. At times, queers have managed to translate gestural language into the very basic building blocks of our cities. Gesture finds its most physical points in buildings that refuse to sit still, obey orders, or tell a simple story of order. Gestural buildings are distorted, distended, and deformed. They break through their skins, move out into space, and speak in ways that are often difficult to understand.[8]

The weaving together of gestures and gestural buildings occurs through the creation of a scrim or choreography of spaces: ". . . it's our capacity to hide ourselves in the mass of life and show our passions behind a scrim or in the shade that has forged the sensibility—and finally, our potential to go beyond that which society sanctions our imaginations to explore."[9] The poses of the body, exaggerated in gesture, move through space and become an activated, staged, and distorted mirror to the productive spaces where one might work or live. These theatrical sequences give us dynamic relationships between spaces that are all for effect, do not lead to some fulfillment in an important function at the end of an axis, and often do nothing else but lead us back to ourselves.

The aesthetics of this choreography of gesture is that of seduction. Accomplished through mirroring and gestures, seduction is the ritualized, socialized expression of desires or urges that we can perhaps never know. It connects one physical body to another, breaking through the complicated divisions our society throws up in its attempts to define orders. Seduction implies placing oneself at risk, opening one's self up in order to entice the other. It also implies giving one's self over to the one doing the seduction. The space of seduction is by its very nature sensual, recalling us to our bodies. In order to seduce, the barriers between bodies have to disappear, the body has to stop hiding behind facades (though the substitution of multiple, distorted facades spreading out like the feathers of a peacock— itself a coded symbol for queerness in certain periods—is part of the act of seduction) and must connect. Seduction expresses itself in architecture through a decorative scheme that covers abstract orders with beautiful patterns that are based on the proportion, curves, and compositions of the body itself. Such ornamentation also has the effect of dissolving walls, floors, and ceilings back into a continuous, sensuous, and experiential environment into which one can sink with voluptuous pleasure.

There is a model for queer space.

The architectural historian Tony Vidler has proposed that we read architecture in terms of the three "scenes" of classical theater.[10]

The first scene is that of tragedy. It is where important stories are told in a setting of classical architecture. They always end in death, as the immutable laws triumph over human frailty.

The second scene is the one we make every day. It is a comic scene, where the vagaries of daily life confront us with ourselves, only to let us lose ourselves in laughter before we go back to our business. Its forms are those of the vernacular.

above left
Figure 1.4a
Sebastiano Serlio,
The Tragic Scene,
c. 1537

above right
Figure 1.4b
Sebastiano Serlio,
The Comic Scene,
c. 1537

The third scene is more difficult to describe. It is the scene of myth, of stories of which you do not know whether they are true or not, where the everyday and the miraculous mix. It takes place in a mixture of the man-made and the natural, the real and the imagined. Ruins and trees create a framework that shows us our own society in a mirror that reveals both its temporality and its order, its natural beauty and its artifice, all wrapped around nymphs, satyrs, and other hybrid creatures.

Figure 1.4c
Sebastiano Serlio,
The Satyric Scene,
c. 1537

I will propose queer space as a kind of third scene, a third place for the third sex, that functions as a counterarchitecture, appropriating, subverting, mirroring, and choreographing the orders of everyday life in new and liberating ways.

I do not mean to imply that only same-sex love can create such a third nature, or that it is the only way to escape from the restrictions of our buildings and the social structures they make real, but only that queer space, because of the particular role we have assigned same-sex love within our society, offers a clear model for such an architectural counterartifice. I will call queer space any space that establishes such a free and real space, no matter the sexual preferences of the persons making it or using it. I will call queer all spaces I think trace a way toward a third nature.

3

Where then does one find examples for such a space? In our society, we have had self-consciously queer spaces for only a little over a century, and even when we try to interpret late-nineteenth-century queer spaces we risk applying standards of interpretation to them that are peculiarly our own, and might be particularly inappropriate to the spaces as they were conceived. The first self-consciously queer space was perhaps Oscar Wilde's home, which appears to us now as a heavily decorated, theatrical, seductive mirror of the owner's own sexuality. Yet it was designed for his family to inhabit. Since the very nature of such spaces makes them almost invisible, as noted above, there are moreover few traces of them. Yet one can find embedded within our society a variety of different queer spaces that have continually questioned, destabilized, ironized, decorated, or just plain queered societies.

These spaces are usually public, mainly because we cannot know the private queer spaces of past ages. The earliest, proto-queer space, however, might be the one that goes back to a time before strict divisions between public and private. This would be the men's and, to a lesser degree, the women's houses that were central institutions of many prehistoric societies and continue to operate in some isolated worlds around the globe.

Figure 1.5
Kanigara
Men's House,
Sepik River
region,
New Guinea

Margaret Mead described one such structure:

In addition to the small men's houses, each village boasts one large men's house or more, built with the effort of several clans, strong enough to stand for many decades if not burned down in an enemy raid, with its attic filled with the great slit gongs, flutes, masks, and all the impressive ritual paraphernalia of the men's cult. Inside the ceremonial house, all the important events of the men's elaborated ritual, war-making, and debating goes on. . . . for initiations and other ceremonies, a great enclosure of leaves is built. Into this, sometimes through a gate itself shaped like a crocodile, the novices are taken, after bullyings, scarifications, and humiliations, to take their place with the adult men in the men's house, which is appropriately enough called a womb. The initiatory myths recount how the sacred noise-making objects were originally discovered by the women, who gave the secret to men, and even entreated the men to kill them so that they, the men, might keep the secrets for all time. Meanwhile, in the great, spacious dwelling-houses the daily life of the village goes on.[11]

The men's and women's houses were where the sexes defined themselves as such. They did this through rituals that connected the body to a larger social network. Thus older men would often have sex with younger men as a way of establishing bonds beyond those of kinship.[12] The same was true for women. These relationships were elaborated in the stories that reverberated through these rooms, and were fixed in symbols, icons, and other signs that had a home in the houses. Sex here united the body and the body politic in the ultimate gesture, one that took place in the amorphous semidarkness of the communal house.[13]

Several observers have cited the men's houses as the earliest generators for a gay community,[14] though of course the definition of such a community is radically different from what it would be in that society. How then did such a gay community fix itself in space? Quite simply by creating a space that had the strange quality of being like an individual hut, only larger, as if it were a dwelling seen in a distorted mirror. These spaces were also closed off, quite secret, and dark, in a deliberate attempt to create an artificial environment that traced the real world and, through its ritualized actions, choreographed it. Often, these spaces were described as uncomfortable physically, as if they were meant to draw our attention back to the reality of our bodies.[15]

The most distinguishing characteristic of such spaces appears to be their lack of internal divisions. What mattered here was the bonding, the gesture of connections, and the creation of an identity through storytelling. Ritual objects, collected with fetishistic fervor, offered a physical anchor to this bonding activity. This was truly a place of myth.

We cannot say much more about men's and women's houses exactly because they were mysterious: they were designed around a sacred and sensual set of activities that may present themselves as something else when an outside observer tries to analyze them. There are also few of them left, so that we can only guess what they looked like from a few societies, mainly in the South Pacific and the Indonesian islands.[16] The men's and women's houses were among the first structures to disappear as the use of space became more rationalized, given over to agricultural and tool production, divided up among productive units and governed by visible, abstract and fixed laws. One observer has noted, speaking about collective houses in general:

> *The collective house represents an important stage in the emergence of the clan and family from the community, a process that has taken many different forms in the course of history. For Western ethnologists concerned with architectural typology, the collective house in its purest form has long represented the dwelling most characteristic of communistic societies in which inequalities and privileged positions do not exist among the family nuclei and, instead, agricultural work is shared equally, as are all other activities. This state of affairs is reflected in the basic features of the collective house: specifically, large dimensions and limited decoration. The dimensions of such a building can be taken as an index of cooperation in the work of construction in which all the members of the collectivity took part. The limited use of decoration may be attributed to the fact that in such societies there is little incentive to competitiveness and, in consequence, little exploitation of myths for family or individual purposes or profit. . . . all of the inhabitants participate in the collective administration of their joint "territory.". . . The fact is, such communities lack what one expects to find in a village: some sort of public edifice for assemblies and ceremonies and the type of building known as a "men's house."[17]*

4

In historical societies, such spaces were often pushed out to the margins of that world. That was certainly the case in classical Greece. There queer spaces were the gymnasium at the edge of the city, and the roofs of houses during annual women's feasts. Both of these spaces served to offer a commentary on the increasingly regulated spaces of the city itself, where laws designated a correct manner of behavior. While the gymnasia were places where boys learned about their bodies and the state through the twin discipline of sport and sex, the feast of Adonia gave women an annual respite from a society that kept them often quite literally imprisoned. In a same-sex situation, they could gossip, make fun of, and create alternatives to a male-dominated city.

We can only speculate about the architecture of the gymnasia, especially since they were originally outdoor spaces where men gathered to engage in the ritualized combination of warfare and bonding we have come to know as sports. It does appear that the gymnasium was no more than a formalization of an outdoor space for running, wrestling, and other "manly" activities. These activities were associated with sacred sites, often including springs, that would connect the body with the particular spirit of a place. The architecture that began to appear at that place then gave a formal presence to what was essentially the open place of appearance where men would wrestle nude with their own limits or their peers.

Figure 1.6a
The Hellenistic Gymnasium of Miletus, Asia Minor, *after 479 B.C. (reconstruction by Fikret Yegül)*

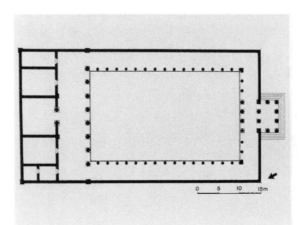

This was Greek architecture reduced to its most elemental forms: the controlled open space defined by the measured march of columns against the rectilinearity of walls.[18] This "palaestra" or colonnaded courtyard had no roof, no subdivided spaces, and no sense of clear function. It marked only an order, just as the naked body revealed its order: body and architecture mirrored each other in space. The word "gymnasium" denoted nakedness.[19]

The gymnasium was a place of sports, which is to say an activity that was not part of the productive world of everyday life, nor directly of the public space of governance. Sports were where myth entered into one's own activities, and where social relations were posed and acted out by its participants, as opposed to the passive experience of the theater. The gymnasium became a place of commentary, a place for the incubation of social structures, and a place where a man might define himself as part of a political environment (the city or polis). They did so in a zone of display, unlike the hidden world of the men's houses. The body itself became the cornerstone for the city. The gymnasium lay at the foundation of that collection of public spaces we think of as the generator of urban culture.

Figure 1.6b
The Hellenistic
Gymnasium of
Miletus,
Asia Minor,
after 479 B.C.
(according to
A. von Gerkan
and F. Krischen)

This was the place where men made love standing up, as if in imitation of the columns, rather than lying down with women. They were equal citizens in this stance. They did not dominate each other, except in age: the younger man would receive the older man, though the free Greek citizen eschewed anal or oral sex in favor of intracrural sex, which involved what one observer has called a mutual friction that is the hallmark of a free democracy.[20]

The queer space of the gymnasium was a place of nakedness, emptiness, abstract order, and the friction of naked bodies. Here, as Richard Sennett has put it, you could find a "choreography of bodies in love. . . . An erotic bond between citizen and city, as between citizen and citizen, is what a body first learned in the gymnasium, an active, upright love." [21] It was an ideal of simplicity and revelation that later architects could only dream of as they tried to address the more complicated demands of civic structures. It was probably the last instance of a place where architecture and the body together made a space in which desire turned back on itself to affirm the presence of a self-conscious group: here sex would liberate you into communal bonds with your peers in an order that was larger than any particular desire or body. It did so at the minimal point of architecture, where the cloaks of appearance were as absent as clothes on the men. There was only space and order itself.

11. In Aphrodite's garden, lecythus, circa 410. London, British Museum (in Furtwängler Reichhold, pl. 78).

Figure 1.7
Vase Depicting Women in Aphrodite's Garden, *c. 410 B.C.*

For women, the free space of the body was considerably more circumscribed. It appeared only once a year, during the Adonia rite, when the women would gather at dusk on the roof.[22] There they would drink, talk, and laugh all night, often making fun of the male world that surrounded them during the harsh daylight.

Women's space was that of the night:

women were associated with the moon, sex with women was something that occurred at night, and night was when the man returned to the home where he had left the woman.[23] All that women could do was to make this time and place their own, and celebrate it. The roof became, and still is in many cultures, the final feminine refuge from the dark, enclosed spaces to which they are assigned in traditional cultures. It is within the confines of the house or compound, so that the woman cannot be accused of trying to escape or make another world for herself. Yet it is also unbounded, open to the sky and sometimes to views of the city. Here women can remain sheltered from others while they remove themselves from the complexity of everyday life.

We can only speculate about exactly what occurred in these flowing spaces, since, unlike men, women rarely celebrated (or were allowed to describe) their own activities. Instead, all we have are the scandalous and self-righteous reports of men who found themselves excluded from the roof and its revelry or contemplative bonding. Women were reputed to make love to each other, but they were also accused of plotting to weave together oppositional bonds that might free them from the nakedly displayed orders of the men's political world.[24]

Certainly the roof became the model for the ephemeral, open, and hard-to-capture women's spaces that persisted throughout Western history. They often became gardens, the *hortus conclusus* where women would await men, tend their gardens (symbolic reflections of their bodies), and create a society through craft and gossip. Inside, they would establish similar spaces. These would be haremlike environments that dissolved the enclosure in which they found themselves into the multiple, diaphanous veils and reflective weavings by which women expressed themselves. We cannot say whether same-sex activities took place in such spaces. We can only observe the existence of such sensuous, inward-turned alternatives to both daily life and male domination and call them queer spaces.[25]

Figure 1.8
Albert Moore,
A Summer Night,
late eighteenth
century

5

The most monumental examples of premodern queer spaces we can point to are the public baths that reached their fullest development in imperial Rome. Modeled on a combination of Greek gymnasia and the caves where early Romans went to find mineral waters they believed to have restorative powers, these places of naked gathering developed into immensely complicated structures that stood at the very heart of Roman society. This is not to say that same-sex activities dominated the world of the baths. When critics assailed the sensuality of these places, as they periodically did, they were more concerned about the presence of female prostitutes and a general atmosphere of self-indulgence that would take good citizens away from their responsibilities.[26]

The baths were not always beautiful places.

They were "bristling with a messy vitality typical of democratic institutions."[27] There was a lot of commerce in these spaces, much as there was in the temples, and there was not a great deal of private space. This was a place where Romans came together, often once a day, in a space where they were free from cares, from rain and sun, from most control, and from the opposite sex:

The experience of the bath—the warm, clear water, the shiny marble surfaces, the steamy atmosphere, the murmuring and echoing of genial sounds, the aroma of perfumed ointments, the intimacy of massage and public nudity—involved the awakening of all the senses. . . . Bathing was also a socially satisfying experience. The cozy warmth of the baths and their class- less world of nudity encouraged friendships and intimacy. For several hours a day, at least, baths took the individual out of his shell and gave him a place in life. It made him share a sensory experience with others and feel good.[28]

These spaces mirrored the body as a social continuum, both real and sensual. Clothes and columns cast off, the Roman citizen could familiarize himself with the old and experiment with the new.

What made the baths queer was first of all their call to the body to return to itself, to enjoy itself and, perhaps, its mirror image. They differed from Greek gymnasia in that this narcissistic aspect of bathing did not extend naturally to sexual acts. Instead, it led to the establishment of social relations. The emergence of such ties among men or among women offered an alternative to the increasingly rational orders of the empire. As a result, the powers of the state became directed toward

Figure 1.9
Sir Lawrence
Alma-Tadema,
A Favorite Custom,
1909

trying to control them by encapsulating them in ever grander structures. The tension between the woven world of sensual sociality and the grand orders of the empire expressed itself in an architecture that opened itself up to innovation. The need to span large areas to allow for the free and sheltered meeting of people led to structural innovations, while the memory of the mystical origins of the baths spoke through their guise as public works.

The result was a place of experimentation. As Fikret Yegül has pointed out:

Not only were the baths an effective testing ground for new ideas, but because of their position between purely utilitarian structures and the more conservative, traditional forms of religious and public architecture (such as temples and basilicas), they were instrumental in bringing widespread acceptance of new ideas and revolutionary styles into the realm of architecture proper. In the grand interiors of the baths, Greek orders were combined with Roman vaults. By accentuating and defining the immense vertical height and curved surfaces of the walls with hard, horizontal cornice lines, by bridging cavernous vaulted expanses with rows of columns and tightly stretched, straight entablatures—in such ways did accessible and familiar forms contain and tame the inaccessible and unfamiliar. [29]

The drama of the baths was unmistakable. Their vaults were so large, and the steam from the water so intense, that they created a dream world where the strict orders defining the public spaces of the rest of the city disappeared. Instead of columns and pediments, there was a surging spectacle of curved spaces that arched far overhead. Instead of a functional floor divided into many different spaces, there were pools of water, massage tables, niches, and benches built into the structure. It was as if architecture, at the very point that human ingenuity could make it larger than life, dissolved into a new kind of nature. As it did, it liberated the body in an environment that seemed to take on its characteristics at a public scale: the half-seen forms of body and building matched each other in curve and bulge, in attenuation of reach and muscled defiance of gravity.

Figure 1.10
Conjectural
Perspective of the
Natatio (Pool),
Baths of Caracalla,
Rome,
212–216

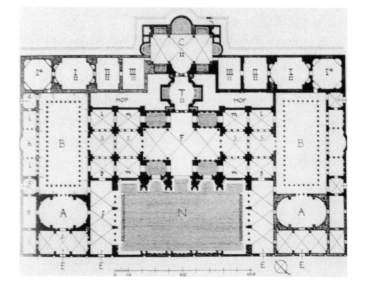

Figure 1.11
Plan of the Baths
of Diocletian,
Rome,
c. 300

While the imperial baths became ever larger, extending out into the landscape to include open fields for exercise in a direct quotation of the Greek gymnasium, some of the emperors themselves sought to create private versions of this place for their own enjoyment. Tiberius built a pleasure ground on the island of Capri, and there indulged in licentious behavior with members of both sexes and all ages in a way that scandalized Romans. Almost every emperor after Augustus, however, had his own pleasure grounds, where the orders that created the humble home of the "first among equals" proliferated into an endless array of columns grouped into exedrae, palaestrae, colonnades, and other tendrils of order. These screens dissolved into a display of nothing but themselves mirrored in the water of pools, plunges, and baths. In the pleasure grounds of the imperial court, order became not the way to hold up the roof of the state or to house its bureaucracy, but a way to measure and accentuate the body in motion and in social relations. Form dissolved into its material essence, found itself mirrored in endless pools, and created endless little spaces for hiding, trysting, or just being sheltered. Order broke down into the mirroring of the body in a new realm of nature recreated by the artifice of architecture. Just as such spaces removed themselves from the everyday realities of the city and the state, so the architecture freed itself from structure and ground, becoming a free-floating collage of sheltering screens set against the quasi-natural backdrop of immense vaults.

Figure 1.12
Canopus Pool,
Hadrian's Villa,
Tivoli,
c. 125

The most notable of these places was Hadrian's
palace, just outside Rome near Tivoli. Hadrian, who became
famous for deifying his young lover, Antinous of Eleusis, created
a palace that seemed to dissolve fixed, functional spaces into
fragmented geometries covering the countryside. There are
little apses and temples everywhere, strung together with long
colonnades. There is no central axis, no great progression to a
throne room (as there had been in Nero's famous palace in
Rome, the Domus Aurea), no wings devoted to bureaucracies.
Freed from the needs of the exercise of power, Hadrian here
created only moments of order, shade, and shadow, where the
body could enjoy itself and the countryside. This was a hedonist
palace, calling the body back to itself and mirroring it in the
isolated, composed fragments of larger orders. Dramatic and
reflective, assembled and devoted to desire, this was a queer
space. Here order stated itself as nothing but a rhetorical
device, revealing itself as only the projection of power
delighting in its own sensual reality.

6

Christians did not care for such space. They did not care for the body at
all, and spent a great deal of time denying its existence or relevance. Instead, they
proposed the heavily ordered, axial spaces of church and state, where rulers controlled
the world with a clarity that demanded that all subjects fit themselves in their forms.

Queer space went underground, persisting only on the fringes of civilization, in repressed desire for certain saints (Saint Sebastian being the most famous), and in places we can only imagine.[30] It became to a large extent anecdotal, which is to say that it was woven together by chance encounters and hearsay. It may also, paradoxically, have become more integrated with the space of everyday life.[31] As John Boswell has pointed out, same-sex love may have been part of bonds in ways that were so normal as to be rarely discussed. In some advanced urban environments, it may even have offered an alternative to traditional kinship structures, and thus may have been prized for the independence it gave queer men. Yet it remained hidden and unspoken in almost all cases.[32]

      This does not mean that there were no queer spaces. Certainly one may describe the great monasteries and nunneries as such. The bare forms of these enclosed environments remind one of the abstraction and clarity of the gymnasia and baths, but here the focus was on the ritualization of the activities of everyday life. Significantly, the body of Christ was thought to be contained within the very forms of the church and the monastery itself, so that the reality of the flesh was embedded in its walls and abstracted into the proportions picked out by architectural detail. When desire escaped from these rigid orders, it created fanciful other worlds, in which orgasmic dreams dissolved the need for the world while, especially in the case of great woman mystics such as Hildegard von Bingen, also eliminating the need for the other, the male, or the inserter in favor of a mystical union of self with self and the universe.[33] That queer acts took place in the real world, in the spaces where there were only members of the same sex gathered together with no outside scrutiny, is almost certain. Abbots and church leaders worried about this constantly (even while some of them lived more or less openly with lovers) and decreed more and more isolated and isolating spaces for the monks and nuns.[34]

Figure 1.13
Monk's Cell

Queer men and, because they were often locked up
or limited in their freedom, queer women had to develop codes
by which they would understand each other, find each other, and
come together. Here queer space takes on its final characteristic:
it becomes an invisible network, a code of behavior or ritualized
language of gestures that traces the activities and places of
everyday life, creating only momentary spaces of union that
disappear almost as soon as the act is consummated.

Such a tracing has no recognizable elements and certainly no monuments through which we might be able to study it. We can only speculate that it occurred in many of the same ways it still does today. Thus queer spaces were traced along routes of trade, commerce, or pilgrimage, escaping from the rigid rules and fixed structures to create relations through space. They offered an alternative to places based on family and state power. Queer spaces became active in the middle of gatherings, such as fairs or marketplaces, and then were found on the margins of the square, in the alley or the hidden corner—places to create a momentary place of satisfaction. Certain way stations along the trading routes or nodes within the social gatherings might gain a reputation for queer acts, and thus inns might provide places of assignation, but of necessity their forms had to be indistinguishable from those where queerness was banned. Queer space was probably always present, but invisible and dissimulating, again like a mirror.

Among the aristocracy,
queer space literally had more room.

Several kings and queens were known for their queer activities, and some, like Edward II, paid dearly for their desires. Again, however, there was no definite place for such desires. They had to take on all the appearance of the ritualized lives of such exalted persons, so that love took the form of vassalage or quasi-political compact. For wealthy women, there was the enclosed garden and the women's quarters mentioned above, where they ironically had more freedom to satisfy their desires than did powerful men, who lived always in public space.

The privatization of queer space thus parallels its disappearance into invisible and ephemeral spaces and matches the disappearance of the body from the discourse of Western society. As culture becomes more and more complicated and the forms that define us as part of the institutions of our society become increasingly large and fixed, sex in general becomes repressed. The church and the palace, the open marketplace and the inn, the straighter and straighter street, the clearer and clearer organization of the facades that line those streets, the subdivision of the house into more and more separate spaces for different activities: all make the self recognize itself not in itself or others, but as part of a larger order over which he or she has little or no control.

Only occasionally, at the edges of the Western world where it is open to "Oriental" influences, does a queer public space appear. Such was certainly the case in the Venice of the Doges:

> *Sensuality was a crucial element in the image of Venice in Europe, and in the Venetians' sense of themselves. The facades of the great palaces along the Grand Canal were richly ornamented, light reflecting their colors into the rippling water; the buildings were diverse facades but roughly uniform in height so that they composed an unbroken street wall of ornamented color. The canal itself was filled with gondolas which in the Renaissance were often painted in vivid reds, yellows, and blues, rather than the obligatory black, and hung with tapestries and flags woven of gold and silver threads. Christian strictures on bodily pleasure had relaxed in the days of Venetian affluence. There was a flourishing homosexual subculture devoted to cross-dressing, young men lounging in gondolas on the canals wearing nothing but women's jewels.[35]*

This world produced its own reaction, in the form of the spread of disease associated with the arrival of foreigners into the ports, and as a result also produced the first places of isolation—ghettos. Venice is where syphilis first appeared in Europe, and its spread became associated with licentious behavior that had to be contained.[36]

Figure 1.14
Christopher
Brown,
Untitled (Porthole),
1993

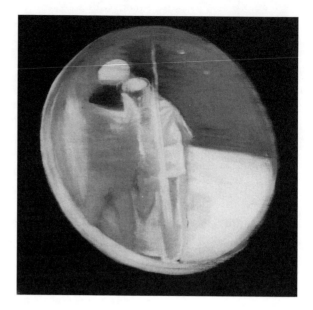

7

There were, however, some places where queer space could exist—at least as far as we can ascertain from anecdotal history or some court proceedings. Ships, those structures that bring another world to cities such as Venice, were places where same-sex acts notoriously flourished. Most observers see this as the result of the simple absence of women on many, especially military, vessels. Though this condition undoubtedly played a part in encouraging same-sex activities, there was also something about ships that created a certain freedom from the norms of the everyday, opening up a space of freedom exactly within the most confined condensations of technology and the ritualized military order that expressed itself through such craft. Ships were floating pieces of society, always slightly unhinged from the norm. The queer space of the boat was a floating one, as if order had become a fragment. It was one in which the body was exposed to the elements. It was a condensed version of the world. In all these ways, it encouraged homosexuality.

The space of the boat itself was rather queer.

It was continuously curved, and had few of the axes and orders that marked the organization of cities and buildings on land. Sleeping quarters resembled the tight and cellular spaces of the men's houses, arched together by the beams of the boat. There was no distinct or separate private or public space, except for the rooms of the officers, and all life was lived out in the open. Men accepted the deformed geometries and tight confines of the boat because it was meant to be functional. The vessel itself was a body cruising through the water. It was also a body that contained a society. The result was a queer space that always curved back on itself, that enforced contact, that reminded one of the fragility and the muscularity of the body.[37]

The other notoriously queer space was that of confinement, whether prisons or the boys' and girls' schools that began to appear in the sixteenth century as an annex to monasteries and nunneries. The prison was, of course, the place where the naked power of institutional order revealed itself most clearly. Here there was no pretense about function or beauty, only the act of confinement that removed the person from the outside world and kept all views of the outside world in. Here the body was under surveillance, including the closest possible form of such an exercise of power, rape. At the same time, the body could resist the cells, the grates, and the walls by creating a body with other bodies. Turning back to the irreducible fact of its existence, it could create bonds of desire that no state authority could control.[38]

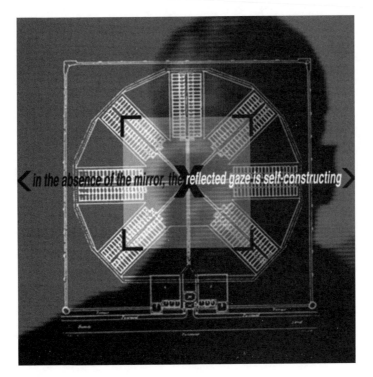

in the absence of the mirror, the reflected gaze is self-constructing

Figure 1.15
Steve Jaycox,
Prison Interior,
1966

Figure 1.16
Giovanni Battista
Piranesi,
*The Round Tower
(State V),*
from the *Carceri,*
c. 1770

Again, the spaces where such acts take place were queer. They are deformed, theatrical versions of the orders inherent in the buildings of normal, everyday use. They were the fortresses that didn't keep the outside out, but kept one imprisoned, thus mapping out the interiorization of the fear of the outside into forms of deformed self-definition. Inside a prison, the gridded structure, strong walls, and regulated openings that were meant to be part of any "correct" architecture became correctional, enforcing their own rhythms on the body.

Prisons were the ob-scene, the hidden or backstage reality of the social scene. They were the hidden reality of order. They were also expressive of order in their very composition. They were extreme in their reduction of light and scale. Prison walls towered over you, spaces pushed in on you, and all relative scale disappeared. Only the bonds themselves appeared. They pushed the act of seeing as a way of controlling the world to an expressive extreme. In the famous images Piranesi created of the prison at the moment that it became a rationalized institution, its forms turned back on themselves in dark spirals and expanded to create a space that, though seemingly rationally constructed, is impossible to comprehend.[39] Only the knowledge of the body, living out its pain and desire, could stand against these constraints. The prison, then, was the queer space where the self was forced to confront his or her own body without relation to social relations, without the relative comfort of everyday life, and without escape. The mirror always became a dark hole sucking you into itself.

The school was an altogether different place. Though this was and still is often a place of confinement, and a place where order revealed itself in all of its naked power, thus creating a staged version of the artifice to which we subject ourselves, it was also consciously a place of acculturation. Based on the Greek gymnasium, the male boarding school especially often existed on the very outskirts of civilization, outside small villages. It was surrounded by large playing fields where the future citizen defined himself through the exertions of his body. Its architecture crossed the domestic forms of the house with the large public spaces of classroom and chapel.

Figure 1.17
Dormitory at the Collège de Navarre, *seventeenth century*

49

These elements were based on prototypes one can find in the monastery, thus creating a symbiotic relationship between public and private that often confused the two. There were barracks where all slept together, and baths for communal cleaning. The only visible order was that of the white walls against which bodies stood out. In what was both home and place of gathering, the scene and the obscene mingled.[40]

Within such a setting, the boy was supposed to become part of the culture not just through learning, but through the creation of close bonds with his fellow students. It is then not surprising that intimate knowledge became the basis of many "old school ties." This appears to be less the case with women's schools, because there was no need to create future elites bonded through mutual pleasure, secrecy, or ritualized body knowledge. The boy's school became a model for the creation of a coherent elite, and part of that act was quite often carnal knowledge. This process was probably reinforced by the coincidence of puberty and the acquisition of knowledge, so that carnal and mental constructions became bound up together. That such experiences were later usually repressed did not prevent them from becoming a vital part of the culture, especially in England. This was also because the boarding school created a mythological version of society, in which its rules and regulations became rituals strung together by gestural behavior. Young boys were initiated into male cults, and secret societies with obscure signals flourished. These coteries mirrored the militaristic and class-based society on the outside in a condensed and easy-to-comprehend manner. Thus the space of the boarding school became the queer and repressed base for a normal and normative society.[41]

8

The final defense of queer space and of the body was perversity.

Transgressive acts allowed the body and the self to escape the confines of society and create their own, perverse space. Sadomasochism, cross-dressing, and bestiality may not have been part of the everyday life of most citizens of the Western world during the last millennium, but, if the collections of "The Heavens" in the Bibliothèque Nationale in Paris (the repositories of materials the authorities deemed pornographic or seditious) are any indication, they were, by the eighteenth century in a country such as France, an integral part of the lives of at least part of the population. This was the aristocracy that had removed itself from most of the cares of everyday life, living off the proceeds of lands managed by others, or isolated in the capital or at the court. Theirs was a subculture that had cut itself loose from most of the bounds that still contained the rest of society. Their architecture was perverse and even queer.

The outrageously rich "hotels" and palaces expressed their newfound freedom, emphasizing as they did a mixture of material sensuality in the endlessly worked gilt and lacquered surfaces that piled on top of each other to create deeply layered forms, with the heroic orders of columns that became doubled and tripled into layered pilasters with no function. These muscled weavings of classical elements held up wedding cakes of architraves that would then support a ceiling painted to make it dissolve into the ether. These interiors were layered perversions of architectural forms, ephemeral in their appearance, free of constraints, and luxurious in their sensual appeal to the body they mirrored in their curves.

The salons of the most refined members of the French aristocracy exhibited all of the attributes of queer space. The walls became mirrors, the orders became rhetorical, the surfaces became sensual, the furnishings were collections of pieces gathered out of materials from all over the world to create a theatrical composition that mimicked the body and the orders that contained it in a deformed manner that emphasized certain aspects of the body while making the rest of it disappear into the folds of drapery. English observers and some French moralists decried such spaces as being decadent and effeminate,[42] and certainly the clarity of definition of form, function, and social role here started to fall apart.

Figure 1.18
François de Cuvilliés, Spiegelsaal in the Amalienburg, Nymphenburg, Munich, *1734–1739*

The most extreme version of such an environment merely took the next step by revealing the body and its desires within the space. *Fanny Hill*[43] in England and, most famously, *The 120 Days of Sodom*[44] in France reveled in the fantastic implications of the overdesigned salon. Peepholes would give the viewer a view into a place where drapes and clothes only half cloaked the figures of desire—but also, as several observers have pointed out, opened the viewer up to attack from behind, thus erasing the aesthetic distance so necessary to the enjoyment of normal spaces and acts.[45] The layers of enclosure themselves, having dissolved from walls and columns into drapes, bedsteads, and clothes, only had to be peeled away to reveal the body that was already present. Quite often, that body was one of the same sex, but gender mattered little in this voluptuous maelstrom of self-destructive desire.

The palace the Marquis de Sade imagined in his story was the Xanadu of all such places of desire. He placed it at the very edge of civilization, and, in fact, removed from it on an inaccessible mountaintop. Outside the bounds of society, anything could happen. The pleasure palace itself was a castle, as if reminding the aristocrats who retired to it of the roots of such places and their wealth. Here power in its origins and isolation revealed itself. The castle was voracious, sucking into itself not only the objects of desire, but also provisions and luxury items from all around the world. Here the perverse friends could be among themselves and indulge in their most outrageous fantasies.

At its heart was the salon of seductions, itself a parody of throne room, theater, prison, school, closet, and bath all cast in the form of an aristocratic salon:

> *Its shape was semicircular; set into the curving wall were four niches whose surfaces were faced with large mirrors, and each was provided with an excellent ottoman; these four recesses were so constructed that each faced the center of the circle; the diameter was formed by a throne . . . intended for the storyteller. . . . she was placed like an actor in a theater, and the audience in their niches found themselves situated as if observing a spectacle in an amphitheater. Steps led down from the throne, upon them were to sit the objects of debauchery brought in to soothe any sensory irritation provoked by the recitals; these several tiers, like the throne, were upholstered in black velvet edged with gold fringe, and the niches were furnished with similar and likewise enriched material, but in color dark blue. At the back of each niche was a little door leading to a little closet. . . . On either side of the central throne an isolated column rose to the ceiling; these two columns were designed to support the subject in whom some misconduct might merit correction. All the instruments necessary to meting it out hung from hooks attached to those columns. . . .*[46]

The description goes on to private boudoirs and torture chambers, listing all the accouterments of a well-appointed hotel, here turned into a place of obscenity. It is disturbing how much it resembles the later excesses of self-consciously queer interiors.

What is frightening about this space is how desire turned into violence. The rhetoric of power became perverted not just in the proliferation of stage-setlike interiors, but also in the nonchalance with which the protagonists dispensed with human life. In their continual search for themselves through their pleasure, they must continually assimilate others and then do away with them. Yet they also inflicted pain on themselves, allowing others to enter into them, thus reminding them of the space of their body by the most extreme measures. Here the most luxurious, complete, and artificial world collapsed in on itself by turning on the object of the body that kept escaping from itself. Queer space here was desperate, a place that killed all those that entered into it. Queer space here was the final denial, the black hole into which all architecture, all order, all reasoned notions of self, disappeared.

Thus queer space became a negative.

It became that which is not order, but its perversion, avoidance, or denial. It became not the body in union with the other, but the traces of desire that moved toward a space that could not endure in time and place. It became that which was hidden, drawing us back to ourselves, not as active participants in culture, but as slaves of order, desire, and the body.

Figure 1.19
Anonymous,
Orgy Scene
from the marquis
de Sade's *Justine,*
1761

Chapter 2

Figure 2.1
Oriental
Salon of
6 rue de Moulins,
Paris,
*mid-nineteenth
century*

Aesthetic Escapades
and Escapes

1

The palace named The Delight of the Eyes, *or* The Support of Memory,
*was one entire enchantment. Rarities, collected from every corner of the earth,
were there found in such profusion as to dazzle and confound, but for the order
in which they were arranged. One gallery exhibited the pictures of the celebrated
Mani, and statues that seemed to be alive. Here a well-managed perspective
attracted the sight; there the magic of optics agreeably deceived it; whilst the
naturalist on his part, exhibited in their several classes the various gifts that
Heaven had bestowed on our globe. In a word, Vathek omitted nothing in this
palace, that might gratify the curiosity of those who resorted to it, although he
was not able to satisfy his own; for, of all men, he was the most curious.*[1]

Curiouser and curiouser, the modern queer sinks into decadence. Since he finds few role models in the straight world, and certainly no spaces that affirm his identity or place in the world, he creates fantastic places of the imagination. This artifice becomes so delightful that the outside world can dissolve behind layers of sensuality. Tricks of arrangement stand in for functional orders. The queer space becomes an oasis of consumables composed with the aid of the most refined technology.

Collecting becomes the hallmark of modern queer space. By cruising the world continuously, whether in the imagination or in real life,

the queer brings home to his palace of sensual seductions all the parts and pieces out of which to build his closet world by mirroring himself in the luxury he could afford. That means that you have to be both wealthy enough to afford such goods and divorced enough from one given place to be able to live in artifice. This is what makes the modern queer space the domain of middle-class white men.

Modern queer space starts with the emergence of what we think of as the modern world. It is a quintessential part of the discovery of a new space that is made by man, and in which man makes himself. Instead of having to find one's place in a tribe, working a field or even in a city, a modern person can construct his or her own identity. He or she can use language, knowledge, and, ultimately, money to create such a space. He or she is conscious of doing so, and develops rules for the logical, rational making of his or her personal space.

Figure 2.2
Fernand Pelez,
*Living Room
in Second
Empire Style,*
1862

A particular group of people succeeds better at making such a place than any other: what we call the middle class. Existing in a self-made world of urban scenes and operating through commerce, law, and professional practice, the middle class constructs its own reality as a class. By the end of the nineteenth century, this reality had come to completely define the Western world.

In this world, men created and controlled space, money, and knowledge. Women made the space real within the confines men had established for them. Both could justify their activities and their lives by an appeal to function: the man had to make a living, the woman had to produce the next generation. Only queers had to make a space for themselves, because they could otherwise not survive. They had to build an identity unsanctioned by family, profession, mores, or morals. They had to self-consciously build their own space. Queers were the self-conscious makers of modern middle-class space.

Modern queer space is therefore not a denial, but an affirmation of self as part of culture. The closet is an architectural equivalent of the Freudian mind. It is the hidden interior where we construct ourselves. Contained within the grand structures we have erected, it contains our memories, our secrets, and our fears. Within it, we can create a fantasy landscape that might be grander than anything we can construct in the real world. Yet it also internalizes those same structures, imprisoning us within its most extreme confines. To be able to open up the closet, queers have had to turn it into structures so large, so fantastic, so comfortable, and so filled with mirrors that they can transform those structures from the inside out. The architecture that comes out of this movement has helped liberate all of us from the most restrictive elements of modern middle-class life by living out its implications.

All this means that modern queer space is open only to one segment of the population, and has none of the grand, utopian aspirations and tribal certainties of the civic spaces of the men's houses, gymnasia, boats, or baths. Instead, it seeks to make same-sex desire part of everyday life. It exists mainly in the domestic environ-ment, though it moves beyond its achievements in this realm to impose its vision on larger institutions. In doing so, it domesticates them, making them inhabitable.

One of the places where such modern queer space first appears is in the Netherlands, and in the annals of its courts in the seventeenth century we can find the record of its emergence. A study of these records reveals a network of cruising grounds and assignation points that may have existed for a long time, but only came to light when the authorities clamped down on behavior they now perceived as un-Christian.[2] The word "cruising" derives from a Dutch word, and designates the areas where men would find each other in the burgeoning cities of the Lowlands. It is worth noting that these grounds were often right in the heart of the central institutions of the Dutch state, including the courthouses, the meeting places of the councils, and the stock exchange. It is as if queer men were tracing the very contours of the emerging middle-class society.

Culture played a strong part in securing this new world. As the art historian Svetlana Alpers has pointed out, Dutch art of the period concerned itself with mirroring, mapping, and assembling the real world in a way that would allow the members of this new society to find a place for themselves in the world. It fixed the newly shaped land in a framed and accurate plane that was neither idealized nor removed from the world, but gave it back to the viewer, the owner, or the user of a work of art in an ordered fashion.[3]

This world of representation, in which "seeing is knowing is making,"[4] secured for the new middle class—for that is who controlled this manmade world—a place in the world. The techniques might by now sound familiar: mirroring, posing objects that have been painstakingly collected, creating a world of artifice that is conscious of its very unrooted, artifactural nature. It is therefore not surprising that, tracing the trade routes between cities and gathering at the nodes of financial power of this new society, queer men should come aboveground.

The chronicler of this phenomenon, Theo van der Meer, has pointed out:

> *After a long era in which same-sex behavior predominantly occurred in hierarchical relationships, such as between adults and adolescents, which determined sexual roles, at the end of the seventeenth century this pattern rapidly changed. Same-sex behavior occurred more and more on an equal footing between adults who often would reverse "active" and "passive" roles in the same session. This change was probably due to what Trumbach called a gender revolution that took place in the same period. Patriarchal relationships between the sexes in northwestern Europe—northern France, England and Holland—gave way to egalitarian relationships and marriages based on mutual love and a growing appreciation of women's roles as spouse, mother and guardian of domesticity. Along with the change in same-sex behavior came the emergence in this part of Europe of sodomite subcultures—networks, meeting sites, a sodomite parlance, body language and, without overlooking personal variety, a sodomite role—in which men from all strata of society participated. . . . Gradually, when notions about the existence of two different biological sexes grew, the sodomite, as an effeminate man and a "he-whore," became a third sex, although in official discourse he blamed his condition on his lewd behavior.* [5]

Figure 2.4
Pieter Janssens,
A Dutch Interior,
c. 1660

Thus the emergence of homosexual networks was coincident with the emergence of ideas about personal freedom and mobile social relations in which each person could make a space for himself. It also defined itself in relation to the formulation, based on scientific and moral arguments, of the norm of what the relationships between human beings should be in a society governed by reason. Queer men sought to establish their own relationships within that same framework, arguing to the courts for the first time that they were only following their nature[6] and creating bonds that were mirror images to those between husband and wife—or business partners.

The queer space of the seventeenth-century urban culture then became, like that of society in general, increasingly divided into a private space, in which queer men argued that they were engaged in a mimicking of family or corporate life and should be allowed to enjoy all the sureties of that space, and a private space that was coincident with the public space of the road, the square, and the public institution that was formalizing space outside the private ownership. By activating these two spheres with their bodies, queer men made them noticeable, articulated their contours, and allowed us to understand their contours more precisely.

While the Dutch found themselves faced with the first emergence out of the underground of the network of same-sex desire, queer places began to appear in England and France as well. The courts in England found themselves increasingly preoccupied with raids on "molly houses" and places of assignation on public heaths.[7] In the fluid world of allegiance that mixed business, landownership, and heritage to create a continually changing and vital aristocracy, queer relations seem to have sometimes cemented such points of transition, fashioning intimate bonds between men and women of different classes or backgrounds. The traditional love of one man for another, in which sexual desire may or may not have played a part, became, however, increasingly divided between sexual relations and friendships.[8] Only in the boys' school were such relations still wrapped up in an alternative model for a stable, ordered, and hierarchical society governed by a small group of men who had cemented their relationships through sex and could propagate their shared values beyond the confines of their childhood and its scenes. For the aristocracy, sexual relations became increasingly something one was supposed to have with members of a lower class, while friendship would preclude such desires—a position still articulated by Clive Durham in Forster's *Maurice*[9] two centuries later.[10]

What then was the queer space of the Renaissance and the Enlightenment? So far as it is visible to us, it was the space of the obscene. The creation of an artificial, logical, and utilitarian "scene" for the city, in which proper uses from commerce to statesmanship had their proper places and facades, by its very nature implied the emergence of the obscene, the hidden, the lascivious, and that which could not be contained in one space. This was the space of the brothel and the cruising ground, but also the private boudoir where care of the self turned from narcissism to mirroring in another and indulgence in luxury extended to the use of other bodies.[11]

2

What began to emerge from this matrix of obscenity

at the beginning of the nineteenth century was an altogether different space.

On the basis of a mixture of traditions of the aristocracy and the mirrorings, tracings, and appropriations of the middle classes, it for the first time established a queer space that was visible, identifiable, and distinct. It was the newly established place of privacy, one in which the middle-class citizen could define himself or herself through the object that he or she could collect, pushed to its logical extreme, so that the excess proliferation of such goods covered the structure of the room that was meant to establish a reference point for such an act of self-definition:

The surroundings become a museum of the soul,
an archive of experiences; it reads in them its own history, and is
perennially conscious of itself; the surroundings are the resonance
chamber where its strings render their authentic vibration. And just
as many pieces of furniture are like molds of the human body,
empty forms waiting to receive it. . . . The ultimate meaning of a
harmoniously decorated house is, as we have hinted, to mirror man,
but to mirror him in his ideal being; it is an exaltation of the self.[12]

The dialogue between an architecture established by men and a world ruled by women within this framework, in other words, began to disappear, and with it some of the moral and sexual structures that had kept men and women in their place. The space of collecting, posing, mirroring, and artifactural coherence emerged.

This space was not without social function. As Alan Sinfield has pointed out, the mixture of masculine values and feminine behavior society ascribed to homosexual behavior was a lubricant for an emerging consumer society: "If manliness produced wealth, [homosexual] femininity might show how to consume it elegantly, and how to be a finer human being and more effective citizen."[13] The model of the "feminized space" also provided an answer to a working class that found that the role of work assigned to the man and the place of the family assigned to the woman were being broken apart by the demands of industrialization, which turned the home into a workshop. Here the middle-class queer interior could become a place of definition in a society where that effort was strongly needed.[14] In general, queer space challenged the division of space into places of work and places of living, between men's and women's spheres, and between classes at the very time that laws and urban architecture were defining them.

Queer space provided an alternative model, one in which the act of collecting, posing, and mirroring created a kind of counterspace to the domestic retreat and the place of work because it refused to be either. Instead, it more closely resembled a miniaturized version of such institutions as the museum or the department store, which were then just emerging as the places in which and through which the culture could define itself. These were places where objects were displayed for their own sake, rather than being used, and where a ritualized behavior created a complicated relationship to the space and its objects. By coming into such spaces, you could, just by looking at the objects around you, learn about the nature of your culture, what it had available and what it valued. The space itself removed you from the outside world, but still encouraged public contact, existing somewhere between a living room and a public forum. Desire here became embodied in the objects on display, and your relationship to them had to be one you established by a choreography of poses.

Emerging at about the same time in England, France, and Germany, this space of collecting created the prototype that queer men especially have been imitating for the last century. The first way in which it appeared was by dissolving the actual structure that surrounded the object into a tentlike ephemerality, as if liberating objects that were chosen to reflect a classical continuum.

Figure 2.5
Charles Percier and Pierre Fontaine, *A Bedchamber Design, 1801*

This late neoclassicist, Empire, or Regency movement contained the first great collections of artifacts and turned palaces into quasi-museums. It was pioneered by such designers as Thomas Hope in England and especially by the business and life partners Percier and Fontaine in France. The latter spent their career combining their rigid training in architecture with a talent for social networking to create interiors for the court of Napoleon and the Restoration. In such masterpieces as their redecoration of Fontainebleau for the Empress Josephine, they combined the sense of living continually inside a campaign tent with a gauzy sensuality. Hope covered his narrow and tall English spaces with the same canopy of drapes, softening its rigid lines and creating a space that seemed to exist in a slightly ethereal realm, as if you had peeked behind the heavy curtains of daily life to find a space of fantasy. The carefully coordinated Egyptian, Roman, or Greek artifacts gave this otherworldly space a certain coherence, so that the inhabitant could mirror himself or herself in idealized human forms and luxurious stage sets of a royal life.

This queer space of tents containing a feminized classicism that acted as the setting for an archaeological display quickly became subsumed in mainstream middle-class culture. Queers themselves turned toward a more radical concoction of fantasy to offer an alternative to such normalcy. They began to collect so voraciously that the collections took over the architecture. They created staged versions of their lives that replaced their heritage and social station.

The greatest builder of queer spaces in nineteenth-century England was no doubt William Beckford. Beckford was the son of the richest man in the realm, a self-made entrepreneur who had made his money by exploiting the wealth of the colonies. The young Beckford was both a member of the highest levels of aristocracy (into which his father had married) and a leading example of the rise into power of the trading classes. He was educated at home, and during his whole life was reluctant to leave the domestic environment. He spent most of that life either building the most fantastic version of a home one could imagine or fleeing from the constraints of his home country by traveling around the world.

He did not altogether have a choice in the matter. When he was still quite young, he was repeatedly apprehended in compromising situations with his young cousin William Courtenay, and his sexual preferences precluded his participation in public life. Frustrated in his desires, he turned to other means of expressing them. When he was twenty-six, he published what was to become a classic in Orientalist literature, *Vathek*.[15] This strange tale of enchantment, sorcery, and frustrated power is a parable of what happens to those who engage purely in gluttony and a search for power, rather than seeking what is true and beautiful. The language of the tale tells a different story, as it luxuriates in the very sensuality it seeks to overcome. The spaces of *Vathek* are rich, but vague. They are fairy-tale palaces and dark dungeons where the specifics of everyday life, structure, or ornament fall away in layers of atmosphere.[16]

In 1796, Beckford set out to build himself a retreat or pleasure palace. It was to become the grandest home in England, and perhaps its most idiosyncratic. Beckford located it in the wilds of the countryside, thereby placing himself consciously at the edges of civilization. The house, called Fonthill, was meant to evoke an abbey that once stood on the site, and the whole design, from the hand of James Wyatt, was a Gothic fantasy that spread out in a giant cross over its site, sending buttresses and turrets out to meet the primeval forest. Its central feature was a tower so difficult to build that it collapsed on several occasions. This 276-foot-high exclamation point in the landscape had no particular function, and it is difficult to avoid a phallic reading of its form, especially since Beckford made a similar shape a central part of his second home in Bath.[17]

Figure 2.6
John Martin,
*View of the
South Front
of Fonthill
Abbey,*
after 1815

The real marvel of Fonthill came inside. If the outside of the building was slightly mysterious, threatening, and alien, as if to keep outsiders away (and Beckford isolated himself from society), then the inside was an almost absurdly rich pageant of color and texture. Room after room spread out throughout the castle, each one filled with myriad objects. The Oak Parlor, for instance, was one of Beckford's favorite spots in his house:

> It was made somewhat dark and gloomy by the colonnade which shaded the south windows and by the oblique cross light coming from the west oriel window. Moreover the ceiling was low and the walls were hung with family portraits and tapestry. Below the portraits concealed doors in the wainscot opened into water-closets. When alone or with a few hangers-on Beckford dined in the Oak Parlour, always in state. In the projecting Nelson Turret a winding stairway led to the floor above. It contained the adjacent Yellow Withdrawing Rooms over the Oak Parlour, and the Gothic Cabinet with walls of green silk, inset mirrors and ceiling of fan tracery.[18]

This combination of gloom and richness made the whole environment appear to both glow and recede into the depths. What gave you a sense of place was the markers of a lineage, rhetorically placed all around you to remind you that this son of a *parvenu* had a place in the social structure, and a physical structure that was so overscaled as to overwhelm you. The materials then clothed this highly artificial framework with pure luxury:

> *Whereas Wyatt, who prided himself on a correct understanding of the English Gothic style, would invariably, when left to his own devices, use pastel shades, and at the boldest a Pompeian red, Beckford, who thought nothing of mixing continental with English styles, favoured the conjunction of exotic crimson, scarlet, purple and gold decoration. Such oriental colour schemes were at least twenty years in advance of the Prince Regent's decoration of the Brighton Pavilion.*[19]

What Beckford established as his interior became a hallmark for queer spaces. First, it was based on deliberately exotic sources, whether medieval or Oriental, so that it established itself as another world, parallel to, older than, and perhaps better than the real world outside the door. Second, that world was paradoxically shot through with elements that would establish its roots, its reality, and its power, as if the owner wanted to pose his power to control this space, to be conscious of its artificial nature, and to manipulate the viewer's reactions. Third, the interior was filled with vast collections. Beckford was the first true antiquarian in England, and his collections of French furniture and tapestries, as well as his library, became the basis for some of the greatest public and private displays in the country.[20]

Figure 2.7
James Wyatt,
St. Michael's
Gallery,
Fonthill Abbey,
Wiltshire,
1812

He was a consummate connoisseur who spent his whole life honing his ability to judge what had once been objects of everyday use and were now, by the very act of collecting, turned into art objects. Out of all of these elements, Beckford created an enclosed world that defined him in opposition and in tenuous relation to the world around him.

The result was indeed a fantastic place. It was the fulfillment of a vision Beckford had had at the time he wrote *Vathek* of what his life could be like at Fonthill:

> . . .the line of apartments and apparently endless passages extending from it on either side were all vaulted—an interminable stair case, which when you looked down it—appeared as deep as the well in the pyramid—and when you looked up—was lost in vapour, led to suites of stately apartments gleaming with marble pavements—as polished as glass—and gawdy ceilings. . . . Delightful indeed were these romantic wanderings—delightful the strayings about this little interior world of exclusive happiness surrounded by lovely beings, in all the freshness of their early bloom, so fitted to enjoy it. Here, nothing was dull or vapid—here, nothing resembled in the least the common forms and usages, the "train-train" and routine of fashionable existence—all was essence—the slightest approach to sameness was here untolerated— monotony of every kind was banished. Even the uniform splendour of gilded roofs—was partially obscured by the vapour of wood aloes ascending in wreaths from cassolettes placed low on the silken carpets in porcelain salvers of the richest japan. The delirium of delight into which our young and fervid bosoms were cast by such a combination of seductive influences may be conceived but too easily. . . . The glowing haze investing every object, the mystic occasioned so bewildering an effect that it became impossible for any one to define—at the moment— where he stood, where he had been, or to whither he was wandering— such was the confusion—the perplexity so many illuminated storeys of infinitely varied apartments gave rise to. It was, in short, the realization of romance in its most extravagant intensity.[21]

Figure 2.8
Peter Herwegen,
Minstrel Hall,
Neuschwanstein
Castle, Bavaria,
1869

Beckford built his "Delight of the Eyes" or "Support of Memory." Unfortunately, the effort depleted his considerable bank accounts, and he had to sell Fonthill and his collections—realizing a profit that allowed him to build Landsdowne, his castle in Bath. Fonthill remained as the symbol of a collector's folly, the very emblem of the acquisitive, self-defining new middle class. Because it was outside the mainstream of that class, since it was larger, more distant, and more outrageous—queerer—than the more modest homes they created for themselves, it served as such an iconic touchstone replicated in smaller scales throughout the parlors of the realm.

A few decades later, the King Ludwig II of Bavaria set out on a similar mission. Since he was a king and not a commoner, he could command the resources that allowed him to build not one but four grand palaces, each more outrageous than the last. Yet in the end he was exiled, bankrupted, and eventually even killed by his desires. That these desires focused on men is today in little doubt, as is the fact that the spaces he designed became icons to which the middle class still turns today as the embodiment of fantasy: Disney's Magic Castle is based on Ludwig's Neuschwanstein Castle.[22]

Ludwig II was a strong supporter of Richard Wagner, and sought to build an opera house in Munich for his use. From Wagner he seems to have derived the idea of building a *Gesamtkunstwerk* as a stage set in which he could fulfill his royal destiny. Not content to rule within the parameters set out for him, he seems to have spent his whole life trying to create the proper setting that might validate his life. This included the neomedieval Neuschwanstein Castle, an extension of an earlier hunting lodge that by association would make him into a Holy Roman Emperor, and a replica of Versailles that would cement his bonds to his distant Bourbon family members.[23]

His first architectural act was the creation of a winter garden at the family palace in Munich. This was a fantastic realm made even more convincing by a local scene painter. This jungle offered the teenage king an escape and countermodel to the constraints of state. As he became increasingly alienated from both power and the culture of Munich, however, he removed himself from modernity, the city, and the concerns of state. The first castle he

created was that at Neuschwanstein, which he began in 1869. Though the castle was meant to be medieval in appearance, its interiors were eclectic and tended to an Oriental theme that justified the proliferation of objects, soft surfaces, and decorative overlays. At the heart of this pleasure palace were a peacock throne and a Moorish retreat.

The luxury of these interiors continued in Ludwig's largest construction, Herrenchiemsee Castle. This was the replica of Versailles. Here the baroque format of the palace tended in almost every room toward the rococo decoration with which the king had grown up in Munich, thus merging the comfortable and voluptuous forms of his childhood with the theater of royal grandeur to which he aspired.

Figure 2.9a
Peter Herwegen,
King's Bedroom,
Neuschwanstein
Castle, Bavaria,
1869

Figure 2.9b
Georg Dollmann,
State Bed-
chamber,
Herrenchiemsee
Castle, Bavaria,
1878

What set Ludwig's work apart from most other fantastical environments was his search for historical accuracy, which somehow managed to coincide with his thirst for sensual luxury:

> For the King, however, what mattered was not just the achievement of the broad theatrical effect he had seen prefigured in sets for Wagner's operas or plays about La Pompadour; he was also deeply concerned with details of historical accuracy, and merciless with criticism when able to detect some departure from the photographs or prints used as models by his designers. He was particularly scathing about any lapse from dignity in representations of his royal heroes. Many of Ludwig's interventions were caused by his sensual appetite for colours and materials, which were both rich and gaudy.[24]

Paradoxically, the thirst for historical accuracy and the need to indulge himself seem to have merged in the creation of this complete environment:

> Ludwig did not admit earlier works of art into his castles. Apart from an 18th-century clock in the Mirror Room at Linderhof almost everything in all his buildings was made directly under his aegis. The decorative ensembles were a direct projection of his personality and no alien artifacts carrying undisciplined memories and meanings would be allowed to intrude upon their absolutist egocentricity. For the same reason he did not collect contemporary works.[25]

The palaces he created were thus self-contained artifacts through which he could define himself. Mirroring, mapping, posing, and the self-conscious creation of an artificial world have not yet found a grander expression. It is perhaps inevitable that Ludwig became a virtual prisoner of his palaces, though later in life he preferred the smaller creation of Berg Castle, where he died by drowning (in good romantic fashion) after he had been deposed.

Figure 2.10
Hans Breling,
The Interior of the Moorish Kiosk at Linderhof Castle,
after 1874

3

If Ludwig II and William Beckford represented the grand makers of queer interiors of a scale and intensity that it would of necessity be almost impossible to imitate, Jean Des Esseintes, the fictional character at the heart of J.-K. Huysmans's *A Rebours* (*Against Nature*), and the very real Oscar Wilde represented the merger of such ambitions with the tradition of ephemeral, tentlike structures at a scale in which the middle class could imagine living. They set the tone for an aestheticizing or queering of middle-class impulses, one that married culture and home to create a sensual escape from the world of commerce. This aestheticism

> *presents the interior as a place where the man of imagination can seal himself off from the philistine world, surround himself with sensuous objects and cultivate what bourgeois culture deemed his "feminine" self— his aesthetic sensibility. Yet a retreat to the feminine realm seems invariably to mean a loss of ego autonomy, a slide into self-destruction.*[26]

This self-destruction is solved—when it does not lead to frustration or literal death—by placing the body at play, as the intermediary between pleasure and consciousness, the converter of one into the other. Aestheticism poses our capacity to enjoy[27] the materiality of the world as an answer to rational, logical structures that remove us from the world.

Jean Des Esseintes, the effeminate and highly refined scion of an old family, epitomizes the failure of a world of artifice that turns in on itself. Des Esseintes at first uses his considerable fortune to create oases of sensuous luxury:

> This room where mirror echoed mirror, and every wall reflected an endless succession of pink boudoirs, had been the talk of all his mistresses, who loved steeping their nakedness in this warm bath of rosy light and breathing in the aromatic odours given off by the camphor. But quite apart from the beneficial effect which this tinted atmosphere had in bringing a ruddy flush to complexions worn and discoloured by the habitual use of cosmetics and the habitual abuse of the night hours, he himself enjoyed, in this voluptuous setting, peculiar satisfactions—pleasures which were in a way heightened and intensified by the recollection of past afflictions and bygone troubles.[28]

This height of artifice soon becomes troubling to him, and with it the notions of sociality and "normal" sexuality, both of which seemed bound up with each other. Des Esseintes seeks to flee, but, since he still believes that "artifice. . . to be the distinctive mark of human genius,"[29] it is not into nature or the past, but into a highly refined version of the domestic interior:

> Already he had begun dreaming of a refined Thebaid, a desert hermitage equipped with all modern conveniences, a snugly heated ark on dry land in which he might take refuge from the incessant deluge of human stupidity. One passion and one only—woman—might have arrested the universal contempt that was taking hold of him, but that passion like the rest had been exhausted.[30]

Figure 2.12
Drawing Room,
Robert Edis
House, London,
c. 1870

The house he designs is a collector's palace filled with furnishings and pictures. One room is all red, another "the colour of a cigar box," and each is more refined than the next.[31] This abstraction of luxury is punctuated with works of art that represent human suffering in its many stages, as if in a de Sadean memory of his own body, real and always decaying, to which his return to an (artificial) home brought him back. His bedroom was, in fact, the ultimate reversal of the layers of luxury that he had draped around himself:

> After turning the question over in his mind, he eventually came to the conclusion that what he should try to do was this: to employ cheerful means to attain a drab end, or rather, to impress on the room as a whole, treated in this way, a certain elegance and distinction, while yet preserving its essential ugliness. He decided, in fact, to reverse the optical illusion of the stage, where cheap finery plays the part of rich and costly fabrics; to achieve precisely the opposite effect, by using magnificent materials to give the impression of old rags; in short, to fit up a Trappist's cell that would look like the genuine article, but would of course be nothing of the sort.[32]

Even this reduction into abstraction is not enough, and Des Esseintes flees first into the collecting of flowers, then just scents, and finally finds satisfaction, after he has found himself "turning female,"[33] in regular enemas, before abandoning his search for self-reconstruction altogether.

Des Esseintes' house is the tragic side of middle-class queer space, one that fails to create a space that validates itself. The pieces and parts of that interior, from the red wallpaper to the monk's cell to the images of suffering men, became mainstays of the queer interior, and remind us always that

the making of a middle-class queer space is one that is always against nature:

against the body, against reality, against the everyday space society makes and remakes around the queer mirror.

At around the same time, Oscar Wilde articulated a space for what now was called homosexuality as clearly and positively as he established the definition of that life in his passionate defense of his behavior at his famous trial of 1895. To Wilde, the artifice of the interior was the building block of culture, exactly because it referred the body back to itself through gesture and referred the culture back to the activity or craft of making that might reconnect the middle class with a sense of reality.

In this way, Wilde brought to a head a long tradition of dandyism. To him, it became a way of seeing the work of design as the expression of a newly free individual who lived in a world not of sordid reality, but only of appearances. It was the task of the artist or architect to reduce to pure planes of color. This abstract world was as modernist as anything imagined by Mondrian half a century later, but had none of his aspirations of a total transformation of reality. Freedom in a world of pure sensation was all that was necessary.[34]

The free-floating exhibitionist perusing the new scenes of the cities was already a figure celebrated in art and fiction. What Wilde brought to that tradition was a sense of queer self-consciousness:

> *One major departure of Wilde's dandyism from its Regency predecessor was the addition of a homoerotic presence. Previous versions of dandyism often drew suspicion from those who viewed the dandy's sometime effeminacy as peculiar, but these never possessed more than the most unclear and seemingly implausible allusions to the love that dare not speak its name. Rather, the dandies' effeminacy was attributed to a disinterest in sex, not to an interest in same-sex activity. It was Wilde who transformed dandyism into a vehicle for a homoerotic presence and a sexualized symbol of the Decadence, marking his version as radically different from those of the past.[35]*

According to some recent observers, Wilde's achievement was to meld the body, art, and the artifice of interior in one form and, in fact, a person: the gestures of the body became a construct that allowed the homosexual to define himself in space, turning himself into an actor capable of holding an audience, attract other men into the play of movements, and inhabit a scene that extended his movements:

> *Beginning in 1886, one can trace the development of Wilde's efforts to formulate (at least on paper) a strategy capable of constructing a sign of identity by objectifying homoerotic desire and situating it on the surfaces of the body of the sexual partner conceived as an art object. Constructing a sign by fixing, stabilizing, and giving permanence to desire was a necessary first step in order to prepare for the appropriation of the sign that would render him as a living work of art while simultaneously bestowing a homosexual identity. The way in which this was accomplished was through a concept of "posing," which . . . represented the highest form of art because it collapsed the distinctions between subject and object.*[36]

Wilde was an actor, a tireless promoter of himself as a living art object who had created himself out of Irish clay into a mirror of the most refined aspirations of middle-class English tastes. At the heart of Wilde's life, at least until his pose sent him into exile (and it was of "posing" as a homosexual that he was accused), was his home. Wilde's house, which he bought in 1884, was located in the then newly fashionable area of Chelsea. With the help of the architect Edward Godwin and possibly the painter James McNeill Whistler, Wilde there created a rich interior in which the walls were painted deep blue and yellow over wainscots of dark mahogany. His own rooms were painted red (for his study) and dark blue (for his bedroom). They veered from the delicately neoclassical to the most luscious Moorish (in the drawing room or den), but everywhere were marked by a profound aestheticism: every object, every doorknob, every piece of china, and every piece of furniture was chosen for the delicacy and intricacy of its design. Instead of wallpaper, Wilde preferred his walls painted, as if they were color themselves. Instead of a suite of furniture of one kind, he chose the best examples of widely divergent styles. It was his sense of proportion, combination, and pose that made all of these pieces cohere.[37]

What makes Wilde's own house, itself an elaboration of his rooms at Cambridge,[38] especially interesting is that they were a queering of a regular middle-class family environment: it was here that Wilde lived with his wife and here that his children, who later provided the most accurate record of the interiors, grew up.[39] The house was also a showcase for his aesthetic theories, which he expounded in highly profitable lecture tours in England and the United States. In these lectures, Wilde made it clear that the objects of everyday use could be aesthetic as well, so that a tea service could be the equal of a painting.[40] In this manner, he unwittingly became the father not only of the aestheticism that he espoused, but also of what Susan Sontag has retroactively called camp, one of whose criteria is that it finds beauty in the elevation of the everyday to the extraordinary: "Camp is the answer to the problem: how to be a dandy in the age of mass culture. . . . The connoisseur of Camp has found more ingenious pleasures. Not in Latin poetry and rare wines and velvet jackets, but in the coarsest, commonest pleasures, in the arts of the masses."[41]

For Wilde, such an appreciation flowed out of a love for the work of the craftsman: "And what is the meaning of this beautiful decoration which we call art? In the first place, it means value to the workman, and it means the pleasure which he must necessarily take in making a thing beautiful."[42] Though this belief clearly derived from Ruskin's call for an appreciation of handicraft, the extreme to which Wilde took it indicates other interests. He commented on how workers were dressed and how they lived as well as what they made, and of course was known to frequent working-class bars for sexual assignations. It was as if Oscar Wilde sought to both escape and ground his middle-class environment, whose contours he sought to dissolve into pure color, through his desires for working-class men and their products.

Another way Wilde sought to structure his world was through a particular brand of aestheticism. Declaring that "the old furniture brought over by the Pilgrims two hundred years ago . . . . is just as good and as beautiful to-day as it was when it first came here,"[43] he called for a reappraisal of the beautiful that already exists in the world and sought to collect those items which had an honest, well-worn beauty within his highly refined environment. As Ludwig II had wrapped himself in royal pageantry, so Wilde sought to ground his world in a middle-class solidity with its own rules and history. He invented the aesthetic mode that Sontag fully analyzed in the essay on camp:

Camp is a vision of the world in terms of style—

but a particular kind of style. It is the love of the exaggerated, the "off," of things-being-what-they-are-not . . . . As a taste in persons, Camp responds particularly to the markedly attenuated and to the strongly exaggerated. The androgyne is certainly one of the great images of Camp sensibility . . . . Here Camp taste draws on the mostly unacknowledged truth of taste: the most refined form of sexual attractiveness (as well as the most refined form of sexual pleasure) consists of going against the grain of one's sex . . . . Thus, the Camp sensibility is one that is alive to a double sense in which some things can be taken. But this is not the familiar split-level construction of a literal meaning, on the one hand, and symbolic meaning, on the other. It is the difference, rather, between the thing as meaning something, anything, and the thing as pure artifice. This comes out clearly in the vulgar use of the word Camp as a verb, "to camp," something that people do. To camp is a mode of seduction—one which employs flamboyant mannerisms susceptible to a double interpretation: gestures full of duplicity, with a witty meaning for cognoscenti and another, more impersonal, for outsiders.[44]

4

Wilde's ideas were hardly original, and he himself acknowledged his debt to the great leaders of the Arts and Crafts movement. It might lead one to wonder about the queerness of that movement, which set the tone for the design of many interiors from the second half of the nineteenth century through the period before the First World War. Several of the leading figures in this movement, including such theoreticians as Walter Pater and Edward Carpenter, were queer (the latter openly and stridently so), and at least one of its leading lights, C. R. Ashbee, was as well. The Arts and Crafts movement, which articulated the highest ideals of how the middle class sought to make a place for itself, found its most extreme expression in an aestheticism that was queer.

Figure 2.13
C. R. Ashbee,
Music Room,
37 Cheyne Walk,
London,
1893–1894

The Arts and Crafts movement called for the integration of craft into everyday life. Against the mass production of objects in factories, which would only give more power to the working class and set the workers against the bourgeoisie who consumed their goods, Arts and Crafts proponents suggested the building of small communities in which the communal making and trading of goods would be an act of self-revelation in material reality. Thus the whole world would be like a parlor, where the feminized appreciation of finished goods and the delight in the useful and the sensual would become externalized into a general condition.[45]

Figure 2.14
Cabinetmakers
of the Guild
of Handicraft,
London,
c. 1901

The site of such communities would be essentially suburban: it would be an in-between place, removed from both the violence and mystery of the city and the wilds of nature, but partaking of the advantages of both. It would be a place where the middle class could establish itself in a middle realm, defined by the making and consuming of artifacts.

      C. R. Ashbee spent a large part of his life trying to fulfill this ideal. Trained as an architect, he became well known through his Arts and Crafts workshops. His "Guild of Handicraft" was a combination school and workshop, into which he brought young men to work collaboratively on interior designs. This was his own little kingdom: "Comradeship was as strong as ever . . . . an idealized group of comrades banded together against the forces of commercialism, which was the normal object of his intellectualized and puritanical emotions."[46] He chose these young men for their freshness and eagerness, which was a quality he also enjoyed in the men he engaged for sexual relations.[47] "The origin of style," he told an audience in 1892, "lies not in the theories, not in the forms, of Art, but in the social relations of men to men."[48]

This world became a reality first in Cheyne Walk, a street in Chelsea where Ashbee lived and worked. There he designed a row of houses that were almost normal and almost antiquarian. They might remind a passerby of the vernacular of the area, but they were all abstracted, cut apart into different levels, and elongated. "Eccentric and affected" was how the newspapers described them. The walls on the inside were at times positively kinky: some were covered with leather and with paintings of prepubescent boys. The peacock, a symbol for the homosexual crowd that was then beginning to define itself around such figures as Carpenter, was everywhere.[49]

At the peak of his success, Ashbee persuaded a good number of his young friends to move to remote Chipping Camden with him. There he eventually established himself and his family in a converted Norman church and created a self-sufficient Arts and Crafts community, the Guild. The site proved a little too distant, and perhaps his ideas had become too extreme: the Guild soon fell on difficult times and eventually disbanded. Ashbee spent the rest of his life as an urban consultant, having abandoned the passion and achievements of his youth. Yet the achievements of the Guild were not forgotten: together with William Morris's workshops, they showed that style could be produced in objects. This meant that a middle-class consumer did not have to build a grand palace or go somewhere to find a proper setting, but could build it up out of objects of everyday use. Ashbee and Wilde connected this impulse with a style that removed one from the ordinary, the useful, and the recognizable, thus queering everyday life.

Figure 2.15
C. R. Ashbee,
Dining Room,
37 Cheyne Walk,
London,
1893–1894

Ashbee's Guild formed a concrete model for a queer community where young men could band together to create an aesthetic mirror of their world. It still echoes today in the by now clichéd dominance of the interior design world by gay men, and by the desire for a retreat to a civilized nature that runs through much queer culture, whether in the taste for clothes or in the actual movement out to resorts and even permanent homes away from the city. It is a desire that mixes the most urban and urbane atmosphere of refinement with a belief that somewhere there is a natural utopia where a queer—and a middle-class man in general—can find fulfillment.[50]

*It is a place called Bohemia,
and it became the natural setting*

for queer men by the turn of the century. This was a
place that was green (a code word for homosexual) and exotic:

> *Within Bohemia are many lesser states. . . . On the shore of the Magic Sea of Dreams lies
> the country of Youth and Romance. . . . free from care or caution. . . . To the eastward
> lie the pleasant groves of Arcady, the dreamland, home of love and poetry. . . . To the south,
> over the long procession of hills lies Vagabondia, [for those who claim]. . . a wilder freedom. . . .
> outlawed or voluntary exile from all restraint. . . . One other district lies hidden and remote,
> locked in the central fastness of Bohemia. Here is the Forest of Arden, whose greenwood holds
> a noble fellowship. . . . It is a little golden world apart, and though it is the most secret,
> it is the most accessible of refuges, so that there are never too many there, and never too few.
> Men go and come from this bright country, but once having been free of the wood, you are
> of the Brotherhood, and recognize your fellows by instinct, and know them, and they know
> you, for what you are. . . . Happy indeed is he who, in his journey of life. . . has found
> his way to the happy forest.[51]*

Here a queer man could reside in his dreams and within his own private
fantasy realm while still functioning within society. If he managed to create an interior,
or a shared space such as club or bar, that evoked Bohemia, he could there live out his
fantasies in the real world. By the end of the nineteenth century, such queer spaces
proliferated around the Western world, giving queer men the opportunity to build a
community of moments within the confines of a straight world. These "artists'
neighborhoods" or retreats of wealthy queers were actual places where queers could
gather and create showcases for themselves. They became the repositories of the most
abstract and aesthetic parts of the Arts and Crafts movement and attempted to create
the gestural freedom of which Oscar Wilde dreamed.

Bohemia was thus not just a retreat. It was also an
experimental laboratory where middle-class culture appropriated
influences and objects from faraway places and times, developed
styles around them, and then produced designs for the straight
world.[52] This was where the grand styles of architecture were
queered, turning them into more sensuous interiors and converting
them into dicta for the making of objects that a middle-class
household could collect. The achievement of the queer side of the
Arts and Crafts movement, then, was to combine a theory about
objects with the evocation of place that established a sellable
and livable setting.

This achievement was, as T. J. Jackson Lears has pointed out, to a large degree "therapeutic": faced with the emergence of a culture they were in danger of no longer controlling, the WASP elite of this country devised several strategies for reasserting their control. One of these was to build up the ideal of the active, natural body, strengthened through its contact with nature: the Teddy Roosevelt model. Paradoxically, another model was aestheticism, which erected a mysterious and spiritual realm of art and religion so intertwined as to become completely obscure for all those who somehow did not have the eye, the feel, or the right training to be able to enter into its hallowed precincts. Thus Wilde's "art for art's sake" could become a bastion of Puritan pleasure that justified itself by claiming to be an artifice that was higher, more ideal, and more universal than any idea about race and class.[53] Somehow the space of a rarefied Bohemian aestheticism did have a romantic connection to the past and to the earth, as was made clear in the work of Ralph Adams Cram and Bertram Grosvenor Goodhue, two perhaps queer partners who queered Gothicism in late-nineteenth-century Boston.

Though Cram was the elder and perhaps queerer of the partners, it was Goodhue who created the perfect image of the aesthetic utopia. He called it Traumburg, and located it in a mystical Germany out of which this imagined village rose, not unlike Neuschwanstein. The village was dominated by a massive, Fonthill-like tower that seemed to transform the cliffs themselves into an exclamation of power, while the little village clung to an organic vernacular that managed to suggest a vague sense of enclosure without defining its contours.

Much of the image of Traumburg became a reality when the firm of Cram, Goodhue, and Ferguson received the commission to expand West Point in 1903. Rising off the cliffs of the Hudson, this all-male bastion became an abstracted Gothic castle opening up into ceremonial spaces that were as rigid as the uniforms the cadets wore. This was the hallmark of the firm, and later of Goodhue alone: stripping Gothicism down to its bare bones, revealing a certain muscularity and vertical straining that seemed to rise out of the ground itself to become a posed artifice of masculine order.[54]

Figure 2.16
Bertram
Grosvenor
Goodhue,
*Perspective of
Saint Kavin's
Church,
Traumburg,
1896*

Figure 2.17
Cram, Goodhue,
and Ferguson,
*Perspective of
the Proposed
Additions to the
Military Academy
at West Point,
New York,
1903*

Cram, on the other hand, tended toward decoration. Fascinated by the darkest and most complicated byways of medieval literature and art, he sought to recreate what he saw as its lush surfaces in modern structures. Thus, in the Church of SS. Peter and Paul he designed with Goodhue in 1895,

> *each tower's upper stages, a riot of rusticated columns, broken pediments, bulbous balusters, and nearly everything else imaginable, rose from a richly sculptured facade whose fantastical detail was very chur-riguieresque in feeling. And the interior, completed by 1898, was even a greater astonishment: filled with fresco, stenciled color decoration, and much elaborate wood and plaster detail, the "reredos wall" at the east end, behind the high altar, was conceived as a baroque fantasia of every other motif ever imaginable—roundels, shells, garlands of fruits, cartouches, and draperies, with putti and angels poised precariously amidst such profusion of detail that the underlying cornice must somewhat have to be taken on faith. And all this in papier-mâché and plaster enriched with gold leaf! (It was, nevertheless, a highly disciplined and effective composition.)*[55]

Figure 2.18
Cram, Goodhue, and Ferguson, Apse of the Church of SS. Peter and Paul, Fall River, Massachusetts, *1895*

Here Gothic styles merged into rococo curlicues, leaving the whole composition to melt into nothing but decoration. Cram went on to design such mainstream buildings as the new Graduate School at Princeton University, and remained during his lifetime devoted to recreating a decorative scheme fleshed out into what he saw as the housing of a monastic brotherhood that would contain the kernel of a new, more just civilization continually resisting the destructive forces of modernization. He thus imagined a kind of queered institution where learning, gathering, and art all became woven together in the integrated shapes of a decorative, organic architecture.[56]

In his writing, he explored the personal side of this social queering of institutions. An aficionado of Gothic tales as well as Gothic buildings, Cram wrote several short stories exploring the world of dreams that seem to well up out of spaces themselves. The protagonists find themselves caught in dark dens of Parisian houses or in the great halls of provincial manors, where the many objects and surfaces come alive and, in the form of a kind of feminized serpents, strangle them. Here Cram seems to be acting out the dark underside of the middle-class achievement in home decoration: the myriad objects it managed to collect from all of the world, objects that, through their age and exoticism, gave a life and a validity to the artificial space they now composed have their revenge.[57]

This is the world of the *unheimlich,* the dark danger that lives not in some distant place, but within the home itself. The most familiar and sheltering aspect of one's life turns out to harbor the deepest danger for the safe and sunny constitution of the self. Here architecture and psychology merge into a fantastical anticomposition. The self mirrors itself in its home, the place that is supposed to make it at home in the world. As soon as it enters this space, however, it finds itself removed from the rational, relational, and ordered world of the outside, and must confront its feminine side, its past, and its own death.

The body comes to one's self in the mirror of the home, and strips away the artifice that allows one to pass through the world. At the very core of the delight in artifice lies its ephemerality, the empty space of the mirror.[58]

The middle-class home, it turns out, has a queer side to it,

one that haunts architecture and literature to this day. Perhaps this difficulty goes back to the very hybrid nature of a movement that wanted to exteriorize the value of the interior (collecting, comfort) and internalize the places and poses of the new city, thus replacing the convenient divisions of inside and outside, and man and woman (as our society had defined them), with the more ephemeral spaces of mirrors, abstract patterns, and poses. If one really mixed what society had designated as the feminine interior and its attributes of common sense and sensuality with the supposedly male notion of creating an ordered, posed reality, one was in danger of confusing one's terms. If one delighted in the artifice of the posed, decorated environment that the culture of the middle class could create, one stood in danger of becoming lost in a web of delightful deceits. If all of reality dissolved into pattern, color, and materials while the body discovered its own life, its mortality, and its desires, the space that would allow one to present one's self in a rational way to other members of society would dissolve. It was a queer dilemma.

On the other hand, the queering of neo-Gothicism also removed the overt references that grounded the movement to a certain nostalgia, abstracting the forms instead into vaguely looming castles that opened up vast spaces below their almost invisible vaults, or presenting buildings that seemed to grow organically out of the ground. It was in this way that a modern space of abstraction and freedom opened up exactly in the deepest recesses of fear and loathing at the heart of the middle-class attempt to create a new home and community. This was the queering of neo-Gothicism (and many other styles, including neo-Romanesque and neo-Moorish) into modernism.

Figure 2.19
Louis Sullivan,
Carson Pirie
Scott Department
Store, Chicago,
1905

5

      Such a queer space did not necessarily have to be a dark space. For some architects and inhabitants, the aesthetic tendrils could become a positive life force that celebrated an Emersonian union with nature breaking through the bounds of civilization. Such was certainly the case with the architect Louis Sullivan. Starting in the early 1880s, Sullivan turned the steel cages that ordered the new center of business activity in the United States, Chicago, back on themselves in ever more voluptuous volutes. Sullivan is credited with a profound modernism for breaking through the classical divisions of building parts in favor of expressing the true nature of construction, but his buildings were more a theatrical celebration of the potential of the new than they were an honest representation.

Figure 2.20
Louis Sullivan,
Hall of the
Auditorium,
Chicago,
1890

The most striking aspect of Sullivan's architecture was its decorative excess. He started by complicating classical columns and pediments into naturalistic friezes, then created escutcheons that he emblazoned over doorways or around windows, posing them over relatively simple facades as explosions of intertwined floral matter. In his two greatest Chicago buildings, the Auditorium of 1889 and the Carson Pirie Scott Department Store of 1905, this decoration took over completely, turning the inside of the theater into an explosion of color and melting the store into a sensuous wave of form that crests over the sidewalk. The viewer becomes overwhelmed by the implied riches of the goods he or she might find inside.

Whether this decoration was based on Sullivan's drawings of naked swims with his male companions, as one biographer has claimed,[59] or on his Irish heritage, as Vincent Scully has always asserted,[60] it functioned as a positive, celebratory version of the decadent, aestheticizing ornament of which designers such as Cram were so fond. Instead of enveloping the viewer and threatening the devolution of form, it seemed to explode out of buildings that Sullivan, over the years, stripped down further and further till it became just plain boxes or simple geometric shapes. It was as if the decorative world of the interior were bursting out of a rhetorically stated representation of order.

Sullivan thought he was creating an "organic" architecture, one that grew naturally out of an elaboration and celebration of the nature of materials and the need of human activity to form a construction that was a natural fact.[61] This was the most extreme artifice: here architecture would create an artifact that was so complete that it would present itself as a piece of a second nature. This object would be then as manly as a real man ("standing tall like a man," in his famous description of a building by Henry Hobson Richardson)[62] and as sensuous as what his society saw a woman as representing; as exotic as a built Bohemia, and as much part of the real world as a business block. Here was a functional queering of architecture, a promise that the rigid forms of an emerging city of business

could be queered into an organic celebration of an all-American, all-natural self.

Sullivan had fewer and fewer chances to live out his ideals as his career declined from an early promise to frustrated hopes, missed commissions, and alcoholism. It was his most gifted employee, Frank Lloyd Wright, who carried on his ideals by integrating them into the emerging form of the suburban home. Wright indeed "broke the box," as he himself claimed,[63] opening the in-between space into a nervous intersection of different forms, levels, and functions that spread out over an undulating lot. Here the queer space of middle-class uncertainty becomes an abstract spatial container. With Wright, moreover, organic architecture becomes a stylistic vision, total and megalomaniac in its pretension of devising rules for the correct construction of a second nature that, when it was built, appeared as alien as any self-consciously new construction. It was up to Wright's stranger disciples to develop the implications of organic architecture.

The strangest and queerest of these was Bruce Goff. A Midwesterner who never strayed much outside his roots in the dust bowl, Goff worked briefly for Wright and saw him as his mentor, but created forms whose extravagance and absurdity took organic architecture right over the top. Goff managed to create a succession of private pleasure palaces in Oklahoma despite his more or less open homosexuality, though this latter "condition" may also have kept him from becoming a more integral part of the cultural mainstream.[64]

Figure 2.21
Bruce Goff,
Interior Pool,
Eugene Bavinger
House,
Norman,
Oklahoma,
1950

Thus Goff pursued his own idiosyncratic path. This led him to design houses that can only be described as bulbous. Not only did they break the box, they threw it out completely, replacing it with flowing, amorphous forms that seemed to live out Cram's worst fantasies. Their forms were often spirals that united the horizontal spread of the domestic structure with a tower-like shape. The Bavinger House, in Norman, Oklahoma, is a good example of this kind of design. It was united by pools of water that made explicit the oceanic motif in Goff's work. Inside, these houses were covered with materials, especially in such luxurious projects as the Joe Price Studio in Bartlesville, Oklahoma, that ranged from coal to goose feathers. The result was that "the enveloping softness is pervasive." [65]

Goff dabbled in surrealism, loved medieval and Oriental forms, and lived a spartan existence in his combination home/studio:

> *Again he was without a kitchen but clearly liked the open, uncluttered space such a location provided. He lined the ceiling with egg crates and the walls with black fabric, and he raised his large, square bed upon a pedestal fashioned from surplus navy lockers. Here he also maintained his office, and here from time to time his assistants also lived in an arrangement one former student described, however inaccurately, as "a small-scale Taliesin."* [66]

Goff's achievement was then to both live and produce an extremely queer vision. This was a warped transformation of anything that American society might recognize as normal, middle-class life. It was an architectural version of the stage life of Liberace. This does not mean that it was merely weird. It means that it drew its strength exactly by applying to the problem of middle-class life and values the queering tendencies of aestheticism. The middle-class collector and manipulator of space for the creation of a self-consciously self-defining new world became the crazed collector, mirrorer, poser, and actor in a fantasy of what life could and should be like beyond the bounds of history and convention. Goff invented a new space. By applying a theatrical dissolution of form into an organic artifice, Goff summed up the promise that one could create a modern queer space.

Figure 2.22
Bruce Goff,
Joe Price Studio,
Bartlesville,
Oklahoma,
1956

Chapter 3

Queering Modernism

1

      It is in the work of two woman designers that we can trace the beginnings of a very different queer space, one that we might comfortably call modernist. This is a space whose contours and arrangements come out of common sense. In the private realm, it is a space that is open, clean, and modern. It is artificial, and delights in its artifice because it believes it represents a saner way of life. Instead of the utopian ideals of mainstream architecture, it presents a domestic version of a modern world. In the public realm, it represents the possibility that the institutions that formalize our social relations don't have to be cold, empty squares or museums for dead values, but can be places of sensuous gathering where bodies might find each other. Yet both of these visions were quickly assimilated into mainstream design efforts, leaving it to the "undesigned" environment to carry forward their implications.

Elsie de Wolfe started her career by clearing out the mess Oscar Wilde had left behind:

> *The [Elsie de Wolfe Residence] became famous not for what Elsie had added, but for what she had removed. She replaced the dark varnished woodwork and the heavily patterned wallpaper with painted walls in light shades of ivory, cream, and pale gray. She took down the velvet draperies and portières that had masked the windows and the doorways between the rooms, and rolled up the extra rugs and carpets that made so many drawing rooms of the day look like adjuncts of a Turkish bazaar. The ponderous chairs and tables that had crowded the rooms were replaced by the lighter designs of the eighteenth century, and the extraordinary clutter that fashionable ladies were expected to amass about them was banished forever as Elsie embraced a new aesthetic of clear surfaces, open spaces, and carefully harmonized patterns and colors.[1]*

Figure 3.2
Elsie de
Wolfe, Dining
Room, Villa
Trianon,
Versailles,
c. 1921

The white room that made de Wolfe famous was no more and no less than the interior version of the modernist dream of a free and open space. If such titanic figures of modern architecture as Le Corbusier and Ludwig Mies van der Rohe dreamed of creating houses as "machines for living in" in which "less is more," de Wolfe did much the same in a sensible way. She got rid of furniture whose scale and complexity made heavy demands on the pocketbook and the time of the newly liberated woman who might have to clean the room. She did away with a world made up of references to the past in favor of the abstractions of empty walls and (relatively) open spaces.

She did this not in the name of modernity, nor did she create sterile environments. She still relied on traditional forms, and believed strongly in copying antique pieces when the original was not available. She had no interest in creating new types. The impulse to create something original had little to do with her belief that an interior should be a comfortable reflection of the way a woman could live. What de Wolfe did invent was the notion of hiding radiators behind wood cases. Technology and the tradition of furnishings both became elements in her repertoire, not facts in themselves: "What she had discovered was not a new style but a new sense of the way a house should function—a synthesis of comfort, practicality, and tradition that would turn out to be precisely what the coming century would crave."[2]

This does not mean that she disappeared into a cloud of white blandness.

In her best work, "formal arrangements were lightened by some witty addition—perhaps a Louis XV footstool covered in leopard skin instead of brocade, or an elegant boudoir where the period furnishings were set off by a bedspread of bold red and white stripes. In Elsie's interiors the harder corners of reality were softened." [3] This wit and eccentricity became doubled in the profusion of mirrors that she used to open up the enclosed space of femininity. These mirrors stood in for the paintings and wallpaper that had previously sited the interior in a wider culture through their references to family, to abstract values told in mythological or religious pictures, or to other places. In the mirror there were only the woman and her friends (de Wolfe rarely mentioned men in any of her books on decorating) [4] reflecting themselves in their white new world. In one of the last houses she designed for herself, de Wolfe took this theme to an extreme by placing a huge tiled bathroom at the center of the house. There she ensconced herself, doing business and her toilet at the same time in a room whose nautical motif turned it into a ship of modernism sailing off into the world.

De Wolfe in many ways invented the modern interior. She started the craze for chintz, that all-purposed decorative fabric that blends all forms together. She dissolved the structure of architecture into white and hid its infrastructure with *trompe l'oeil.* She made interiors that were sensible and sensuous, by and for modern women. Her books popularized the very notion that you could design an interior in a rational and yet commonsensical and pretty manner to the huge audience of newly liberated women. Here was a queer model for middle America, one in which the theatrical creation of a designed interior (de Wolfe had started her career as an actress), made up by a bricolage of artifice mirroring itself in a dissolution of form, allowing for the pose of the body to stand out in contrast, was packaged as a sellable interior.

It is interesting to note that not many women followed in de Wolfe's footsteps. After the 1920s, when several notable woman decorators helped set the tone for domestic arrangements, almost all well-known interior decorators were men. Women have dominated the publications (the "shelter magazines" such as *Architectural Digest* and *House & Garden*) that popularize these spaces, and women make up an army of arrangers, designers, and consultants that set the tone for most middle-class interiors. It is men, however, who design the houses of the rich and receive most of the publicity.

2

We still live in a sexist society. Women can make a place for themselves, but usually still within a structure set by men. Thus de Wolfe's queer achievements became encapsulated, contained, and eventually eviscerated by a mass marketing of standardized decorating tricks. The fate of another great queer woman designer, Julia Morgan, is paradoxical. Though she was not nearly as great a designer as de Wolfe in terms of innovation and originality, she worked within the male profession of architecture and created one of the most enduring monuments to the excesses of male power. Though her work was often deliberately anonymous, she has become a revered model for many woman designers who dismiss de Wolfe as just a decorator.

In her professional life, Morgan was no doubt a pioneer. Yet her architecture was decidedly unoriginal. Throughout her life, she adopted not only a variety of historical styles, but even the mode of such mentors as Bernard Maybeck (who often worked in her office to complete his own commissions). What sets her work apart is something that remains embedded within these conventional forms: an elegance, grace, and sensibility that exactly removes itself from immediate observation. Morgan's architecture passes: it clothes itself correctly, presents an elaborate artifice, and winds up by overstating its plainness. The many buildings she did to house William Randolph Hearst's enterprises, for instance, flaunt their simple facades and matter-of-fact organization.

Only in domestic interiors did she let loose. There "she lavished richly detailed ornament . . . and indulged in a free play of geometry."[5] The other motif that set her apart from her contemporaries was her obsession with pools. She first made her career by designing YWCAs, and the largest space in all of these buildings was a beautifully lit, centrally located pool. But even after she went on to design buildings for men, the allure of water remained central to her work. The greatest spaces at San Simeon, the California version of Neuschwanstein that she designed for Hearst, are the outdoor and indoor pools. It is as if the core of her architecture, behind all the masking, passing, and blending in, is the body itself, delighting in its own reflection as it casts off gravity and structure. For architects such as Le Corbusier, the bathroom and plumbing held central place because of their ability to drain off the reality of the body as quickly, hygienically, and elegantly as possible. To queer designers like de Wolfe and Morgan, the bathtub and pool, the actual space of water, mattered most.

Figure 3.3
Julia Morgan,
Pool,
Berkeley
Women's City
Club,
1929–1930

The queer space of interiorized modernism was thus one that passed as old and anonymous, was white, sensible, and sensuous, highly reflective and posed. It placed the inhabitant within a theater of minimalism, where he or she could make a life. Queer modernism combined two disparate impulses: the drive to create a new world for one's self, perhaps by creating a new self, that lay at the core of much modernist design, and the desire to make one's self at home with the frightening new contours of that new world. For de Wolfe and Morgan, modernism meant that you could manufacture any style in a loose arrangement of pieces, rather than having to evoke a whole, coherent structure. You were free to mirror yourself in a world that kept the violence of nature outside. Structure itself would dissolve, leaving you free to make yourself comfortable while sitting in a nice chair.

Figure 3.4
Private Office
of Jean-Michel
Frank, Paris,
c. 1930

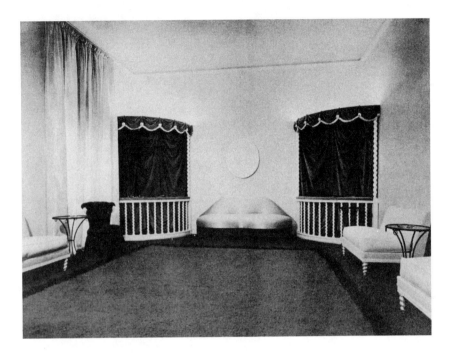

3

There was a surreal undercurrent to such work, one that became a mainstay in the work of many queer interior decorators between the two World Wars. If designers such as Jean-Michel Frank created elongated, deformed, and abstracted versions of classic forms, there was always something haunting about his work. The *unheimlich* spoke through even in his own office. This undercurrent became much more overt in the interiors the rich South American expatriate Charles de Beistegui decreed for himself, first in Paris and then in Venice. He commissioned Le Corbusier to design an apartment for him that made the inside literally outside, on top of a roof, leaving the emblems of domesticity to pose themselves against the Paris skyline. He then assembled a series of interiors, each more theatrical than its predecessor, all of which found their apotheosis in the lavish costume balls he held. There everybody was masked, in drag, and trailing layered clouds of clothes. Furniture, walls, and clothing all came together in a display of light and lightheartedness that confused the senses.

Figure 3.5a Jean-Michel Frank, Cinema and Dance Room, Baron Roland de l'Espée Residence, Paris, *c. 1930*

Figure 3.5b
Jean-Michel
Frank,
Dining Room,
c. 1925

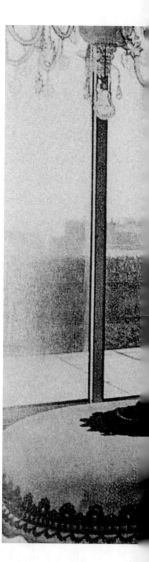

It was among the Bloomsbury set in England that this queer and theatrical mode came into full flower. As the heirs to the aestheticism of Wilde and the Arts and Crafts movement, the designers of this set created interiors that were stage sets for modern living. Rex Whistler, a painter who worked as a set designer and a decorator, drew on Regency models to create tentlike interiors in light colors that threw a web of melting lines over the inhabitants or viewers. His most complete interior was the set of rooms he painted for Sir Philip Sassoon at Port Lympne, Kent, in 1932. The most eccentric designer of the period was Edward James, who created Egyptian harems and surrealistically melting walls with equal aplomb. His interiors at Monkton ran riot with overlapping colors, patterns, and forms that seemed to slide by each other with no apparent relationship. Clough Williams-Ellis, in the manner of William Beckford, created a fantasy village on the Welsh coast (later famous as the set for the television show *The Prisoner*), but his London apartments condensed his classical dreams into the solid shapes of furniture.

Figure 3.6
Le Corbusier,
Apartment of
Charles de
Beistegui,
Paris,
1935

While most decorators engaged merely in a "lightening up" of classical sources, scaling them down and making them more sensible, the queer sensibility was to make things both very small and very large at the same time. These white-washed domestic sets dwarfed the inhabitant while posing him or her. Cecil Beaton caught this sensibility better than any single designer in his photographs of this interior world, and his famous image of Edith Sitwell in her bed is a model for this *Alice's Adventures in Wonderland*–like world. Beaton also realized his images in both residential interiors for the Sitwells and in stage sets that turned baroque forms into meringue while posing characters in all-white reveries.

Beaton's photographs turned everybody into actors in a gauzy world of strange scales and melting surfaces, where mirrors always brought the viewer or the subject back to a doubled and troubled reflection. These photographs, like the images that filled the decorating and shelter magazines, were more to the point than the actual construction of the few rooms for the very wealthy they represented. These were stage sets for the appearance of a smart set, figures who made themselves into deliberate artifices by surrounding themselves with shifting layers of abstracted allusion.

Figure 3.8a
Cecil Beaton,
*Edith Sitwell in
Bed at
Renishaw,
1927*

Figure 3.8b
Oliver Messel,
Messel Suite,
Dorchester
Hotel, London,
c. 1960

The main character of what came to be the dominant tone in high-style interior decoration, carried out by generation after generation of interior decorators, mostly anonymous and predominantly queer, on both sides of the Atlantic, was a mixture of rococo and neoclassical forms that emphasized the deformation of form over the statement of form itself. Instead of stressing structure, columns, door, window, or cornice, it blended all these elements together into overlapping curves or hid them with a continuous flow of fabric or fabriclike coverings. The tone was light and airy, as if the interior wanted to dissolve. Furniture was generally composed, but not all of one piece, and great care was taken to let the artifacts of everyday life, such as small pictures, combs, or books, come into the environment and have their place there. Mirrors often abounded, as did grand gestures such as overscaled chandeliers or sconces. All objects were placed in the middle of the room, so that one did not notice the walls, and the chairs, sofas, and daybeds became actors in this little theater. Textures were sensuous, but again light and often tightly drawn, so that one did not feel as if one was drowning in layers of heavy cloth. It was an interior, in other words, of paradox and wit: a sensible grandeur, a deformed order, a modern familiarity, a grand intimacy.

This sensibility generated a whole industry of designers making sofas that were slightly larger and more accentuated than their historical models, fabric designers creating light but rich materials, antique collectors finding appropriate set pieces that could hold a room when they were removed from their historical setting. It made it acceptable to live in a room that is slightly strange, that revels in the artifice one can collect in the controlled environment of the interior, and that presents a rather perverted mirror of the comfortable middle-class home.

Figure 3.9
Cecil Beaton's Photograph of the Library of Charles de Beistegui, Groussay, near Paris, designed by Emilio Terry, *1930*

4

The influence of such queer styles has become pervasive, especially through the medium of film and television, which has broadcast these stage sets as such. Thus Liberace's living room could become a queer model for the American living room. It has been up to architects, however, to carry the implication of such interiors to their logical extremes and even into public buildings. Queer architects, drawing on the work of decorators as much as on the grand examples of history or great theories, have queered modernism into something much more comfortable than the rigid abstractions decreed by the modern masters, but also stranger exactly because it haunts us with its familiar, domestic qualities.

The most famous of these perverters in this country is Philip Johnson. Throughout his life, this wealthy architect has made a habit of appropriating the styles of other designers, whether architects or decorators, and pushing them so far to the extreme of rhetoric or deformity that they become almost unrecognizable. There has been a method in this manner: starting from the need to make a "home" for himself as a queer man, he created an alternative to the closed boxes of suburbia. By softening or "feminizing" the lines of modernism, neoclassicism, and later deconstructivist forms in the cultural institutions he has designed, he has made them into more acceptable and comfortable, if also less rigorous, embodiments of good taste. He has justified all of this with an intellectual pose based on wit, a denial of fixed principles, and a self-indulgent celebration of his own artifice.[6]

The most famous structure to emerge from his hand is still his Glass House, which he erected on his estate in suburban Connecticut in 1949. This was already a domestication and queering of a high modernist model, Mies van der Rohe's Barcelona Pavilion of 1929. Johnson reduced the house to almost nothing, leaving only the fireplace and chimney as solid forms within a world dissolving into the outdoors. The Glass House was architecture stripped naked, but it was also a box of mirrors that reflected as it revealed. Lying on the leather grids of the Mies van der Rohe furniture, the inhabitant could reveal himself, mirror himself, and control his artificial environment.

Even Johnson could not live in such a queer setting, and he quickly designed actual sleeping quarters next to this statement. Once again, he went to extremes: he buried the bedroom completely, so that it became a queering of the cave into a vaulted chamber covered with raw silk that turned this ultimate Sadean pleasure palace into a shimmering space of closely matched textures, colors, and light. The Glass House and the real house together are probably the most succinct statement of queer space built in this country in the last fifty years. They condense and abstract into their essences the whole history of interior decoration and the impulses of an aesthetic modernism, reducing them to their purest and most sensuous pose.

Figure 3.10
Philip Johnson,
Glass House,
New Canaan,
Connecticut,
1949

Johnson continued to elaborate on his own Fonthill over the years, creating more and more monuments to himself, such as a floating pavilion that makes the inhabitant appear larger than life and, most recently, a visitors' center he calls "The Monsta" that uses the continually molded forms of Frank Gehry to create an emblematically slivered space.

In Johnson's public work, he applied the lessons of decoration to a much grander style. His designs for Lincoln Center glowed in gold and white, melting classical forms into paper-thin, continually flowing arches and domes. His libraries and institutional buildings performed the same eviscerating operation on all manner of classical and vernacular forms. Johnson used brick and stone as no more than thin facades, and delighted in revealing them as masks of respectability. When he built skyscrapers, such as the 1985 Transco Tower in Houston, they became the very essence of phallic power turning into a mirrored denial of form.

Figure 3.11
Philip Johnson,
Sleeping Quarters
for the Glass House,
New Canaan,
Connecticut,
1953

Figure 3.12
Johnson/Burgee,
Architects,
AT&T Building,
New York,
1984

His most famous public building, the 1984 AT&T (now Sony) Building in Manhattan, was perhaps his queerest. It was a corporate office building as a piece of furniture, a Pop Art conflation that marks the importance of interior artifacts as emblems of respectability, here used to cloak the headquarters of a company whose business has no form. Its shapes were elongated and thinned down to the point where they became uncomfortably brittle, yet the whole skin flowed from top to bottom in one sheet of stone. Like any poseur who must pass, the AT&T Building became anonymous at its base, stepping away from the sidewalk while appropriating it as the stage set for the emergence of its own dandified forms. The building's icon was the statue of Mercury ("The Genius of Electricity") that stood in the lobby. Johnson rescued "Golden Boy" from the top of the old AT&T Building, where it had seemed a harmless messenger of profits, and placed it in the middle of the lobby.

There the beautiful youth vaulted through the space,
turning its amply molded behind to the elevator lobby. The executives
would find themselves confronted with its shapes whenever they exited
the building. Johnson had his final queer revenge.

Figure 3.13
Evelyn Beatrice
Longman,
*The Genius of
Electricity,
1916,*
in the lobby
of the AT&T
Building

5

Though Johnson's achievements and politics are at the very least debatable, there is no doubt that he helped liberate a whole generation of architects into a queer sensibility. He made it acceptable to treat the high ideals of modernism as an aesthetic pose. He showed how style could be a mask one could wear, and how buildings could appropriate normal functions for sensual purposes. The generation of postmodern architects he encouraged took his lessons to further extremes. Robert Venturi, Charles Moore, Michael Graves, Robert A. M. Stern, and Charles Jencks made queer forms respectable in mainstream America.

The oldest of this generation was Charles Moore. He was also the one to establish himself most clearly outside Johnson's orbit. Moore began his career in Northern California, where he picked up on the Arts and Crafts traditions that this area had nurtured since the end of the nineteenth century. In many ways, his early work reflects the influence of the so-called Bay Area School, which was in itself a queering of the early Arts and Crafts forms at which designers such as Julia Morgan were so adept into something much more comfortable, understated, and thin.[7] Moore took over the leadership of this movement from Berkeley dean William Wurster and developed it to meet the more exuberant atmosphere of the 1960s. In partnership with Donlyn Lyndon, William Turnbull, and Richard Whitaker, Moore designed dozens of houses that mixed a respect for local building practices with a desire to create free, open spaces. As his biographer put it:

> To home design in particular, Moore has brought a fresh approach to the concept of rooms and the lives we live inside them. This has led him to design open-walled perches, obtuse-and acute-angled walls, columned caves, indoor courtyards and balconies, flying-bridge hallways, and an almost endless variety of indoors levels and paths. From this has come the return of the grand (or giddy) staircase as a major element of design. His interiors are filled with heretofore unknown rainbows of color, a rich and eccentric play of light, both natural and artificial, from every possible source (including windows in unheard-of shapes and positions); and intricate, multilayered transitions between indoor and outdoor space. He has reintroduced visual wit and historical allusion into buildings, and has deliberately used cheap materials or things with "low" associations in highly sophisticated settings.[8]

In Moore's work, domestic reality started to come apart into its constituent parts. The point of a house was no longer to give functional spaces to all the members of the nuclear family or to create a retreat, but to open you up to sensual experience. Paradoxically, this meant that both comfort and the very emblems of house became more clearly stated, as if Moore were creating an operatic celebration of the idea of home:

> *They were not simply variations on the Idea of a House. They were a total rethinking of what domestic space might be, contrived by people suddenly liberated (between 1959 and 1960) from a great deal of their immediate cultural past. Circulation could be vertical, rather than horizontal. Beds could be placed on open lofts instead of in darkened private rooms. Stairs could be turned into seats, tables, stages. All one's furniture could be a part of one's spiralling, ascending or descending Alice-in-Wonderland house. Rooms—enclosable private places, each intended for its own discrete function or occupant—could be dispensed with entirely, in a kind of atavistic return to the Indian hogan or pioneer log cabin or Germanic timbered hearth-and-hall concept of a dwelling. One could bathe in the trees; live like kings and princes in the tiny cabins designed around ten-foot columns and twenty-foot windows. Sunlight could hit you from every angle, winking up, showering down. Glass and opened walls could let in as much of the outside world as you could stand.* [9]

Figure 3.14
Charles Moore,
Living Room
and Entry,
Jobson House,
Palo Colorado,
California,
1961

Charles Moore had brought Bohemia back home.

In such buildings as the Bonham House of 1962 and the Jobson House of 1961, he created collages of comfort. These dissolved the grids and technologies of modern living into little pockets of sensuality framed by abstracted, deformed, and enlarged cutouts of architectural forms. In houses he occupied himself, Moore pushed these notions even further. The first house he designed for himself, in Orinda, California, revolved around a doubled heart of a bed and a shower stall. The center of the house became a doubled shrine of the body. The walls disappeared into sliding garage doors. The house Moore then renovated in New Haven, Connecticut, when he became dean of the Yale School of Architecture (after being denied tenure at Berkeley because of rumors about his sexuality), turned into a labyrinth of cutout screens, each of which had the name of a person, that framed the various scenes of his quasi-domestic life.

Figure 3.15
Charles Moore,
Bonham House,
Santa Cruz,
California,
1962

In Essex, Connecticut, Moore's house featured a shrine to his large collection of toys, while in Los Angeles the house became a rambling staircase doubling as living quarters. All of these "bachelor pads" (which he usually shared with one of his acolytes) were showcases for his talents, but also mirrors of his ebullient, operatic personality. They always centered around three things: a bed, treated as the centerpiece of a stage set; water and bathing facilities; and his collections of artifacts. Together, these three moments of coherence allowed the rest of the environment to ramble off into delightful and fantastic concoctions of form.

Moore's greatest achievement was probably the architecture of Sea Ranch, a condominium complex he designed on the coast north of San Francisco in 1962. Here the domestic forms divorced themselves from the type of the single-family home and became simple loft shapes onto which he then added what he called "saddlebags" that contained all the elements of everyday life.

Figure 3.16b
Bathing Area,
Charles Moore
House,
Orinda,
California,
1962

You would then be free to enjoy the larger space for living. The forms of the buildings mimicked the landscape, abstracting and sharpening them into triangular celebrations of an artificial vernacular. Sea Ranch's centerpiece was not a golf course or a community space, but a swimming pool. Its men's locker room was one of the first sites of "supergraphics" and turned the experience of men being naked together into an almost churchlike celebration of light, texture, and scale.

The influence of Sea Ranch, and of Moore's work in general, was immense. The mile after mile of cedar-sided, sloped-roof residential developments that blanket much of suburbia are all based on this prototype, as are the woodsy ramblings that mark the domiciles of the post-hippie generation. Charles Moore queered the free-flowing forms of modernism into something more familiar and sensual: he made us at home, but at home with abstracted, elongated, brightly colored shapes. His forms might have been comforting, but his spaces were always unstable, devolving into many different levels that he choreographed with virtuoso skill.

In his *The Place of Houses,* written in 1974 as a manual for would-be house builders, Moore presents a queer version of the home. "Rooms," he says, "are unspecific spaces, empty stages for human action, where we perform the rituals and improvisations of living. They provide generalized opportunities for things to happen, and they allow us to do and be what we will."[10] They also provide us with a realization of "the dream of being sheltered and protected." They bring this sense of shelter together with the improvisations of daily life through mapping and collecting,[11] an activity you carry out through gathering artifacts and creating stage sets. This allows you to "camp out" or make a space for yourself.[12] Here was the manual of the self-conscious queer middle-class collector reduced to its most basic ingredients, and turned into a recipe for normal middle-class life.

Figure 3.17
Kent Bloomer,
Moore Man
(Scale Figure),
1975

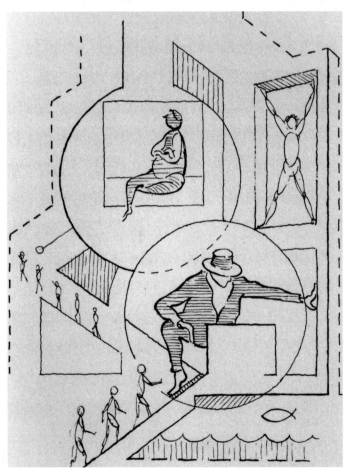

It was a formula that never became stale because to Moore it was perhaps more like a libretto, to be sung alive and out loud by different performers and at different pitches. A sense of theatricality pervaded much of his work. It started from the "aediculas" or little moments of shelter that stood at the heart of most of the houses. These were like children's versions of a home in the world, a place that dignified the inhabitant while opening him or her up to a peek-a-boo game: the bed, the bathroom, or the kitchen could become a stage. The houses would then develop through a series of screens, often brightly colored and festooned with lights, that announced your arrival into another space. They often resembled stages quite closely. At times, this sense of play-acting would explode into arches, layered screens, and dramatic lighting that could turn a simple room into an operatic explosion of flats.

At the core of Moore's design, no matter how repetitive some of his forms became or how easy it turned out to be for mainstream culture to assimilate his sometimes outrageous spatial concoctions into a "developer vernacular," stood a certain sensuality. He had written his Ph.D. thesis at Princeton on the uses of water in architecture, and the experience of bathing or reflecting one's self in water stood, as in the work of Julia Morgan and Elsie de Wolfe, at the heart of many of his buildings:

> Washing, on the other hand, and bathing, have through much of the world's history been regarded not only as activities that can be shared without shame, but even as excuses for relaxed social interaction, and for special architectural effect. The whole act of taking off one's clothes, so as to be especially conscious of one's body and its unencumbered movements, and then relaxing, soothed in a series of monumental spaces—all heightened the sense of being somewhere.[13]

This amorphous, reflective, and sensual heart of space gave
it a life, but the architectural strategy in general was for Moore and
his followers very much a third way that married the conscious place-making
of architecture with the decorative mirroring of the interior tradition,
turning them into an elaborate artifice:

If our century's predominant urge to erect highrise macho objects was nearly spent, I thought we might now be eligible for a fifty-year-long respite of yin, of absorbing and healing and trying to bring out free-standing erections into an inhabitable community. I like that, but am growing impatient with fifty-year swings, and wonder whether a more suitable model for us might be Goldilocks, of Three Bears fame, who found some things (Papa Bear's) too hot or too hard or too big, and other things (Mama Bear's) too cold, too soft, or too small, but still other things (Baby Bear's) just right, inhabitable, as we architects would say. The early modern polemicists disliked the world they saw and expected the opposite to be an improvement (like Goldilocks partway through her testing); but their panacea turned out to have its draw-backs, too, and it seems more accurate to note that, even as humans have yearnings—for place, for roots, for changing sequences of light and space, for order and clarity, for reverie—just so, when each of these yearnings is satisfied, we can feel surfeit, and seek to head another way, to mobility, or ambiguity, or surprise.[14]

Figure 3.19
Interior of
"Howard,"
Charles Moore
House,
New Haven,
Connecticut,
1966

6

In the hands of several East Coast architects, this "mobility, ambiguity and surprise" became a formula for "complexity and contradiction" that turned the queering of modernism into an intellectual game of the highest order. In his pivotal book *Complexity and Contradiction in Architecture*, Robert Venturi made a rousing case for ambivalence:

> *I speak of a complex and contradictory architecture based on the richness and ambiguity of modern experience, including the experience that is inherent in art. . . . I like elements which are hybrid rather than "pure," compromising rather than "clean," distorted rather than "straightforward," ambiguous rather than "articulated," perverse as well as impersonal, boring as well as "interesting," conventional rather than "designed," accommodating rather than excluding, redundant rather than simple, vestigial as well as innovating, inconsistent and equivocal rather than direct and clear. I am for messy vitality over obvious unity. I include the non sequitur and proclaim the duality.*[15]

Venturi mined architectural history for examples of such a sensibility. He found them wherever architects had inflected the grand orders of design toward delight, surprise, and accommodation: stairs that squeezed into small rooms, columns that were too big or too small for the facade they adorned, spaces that undulated away from rigid grids, and decoration that piled up in expressive excess. Venturi loved the complex orders architecture tried to impose on the world, but seemed to delight exactly in their failure: that point where their grand ambitions fell apart either because of internal contradictions or because they had to accommodate themselves to the realities of everyday life.

Having mined history for models, Venturi then proposed his own structures. A 1959 beach house became a distorted version of a child's house, its roof spreading over the landscape and its central chimney rising up twice as high. While his 1962 house for his mother, which became an icon of postmodern architecture, was a similar caricature, here the solid facade that denoted shelter developed a crack right down the middle, through which one could literally enter into the closed domestic world. Inside, a staircase squeezed through space, light came in through overscaled windows, and the whole environment developed in a continual play between forms of shelter inscribed with a fractured system of decoration.

Figure 3.20
Robert Venturi,
Interior,
Vanna Venturi
House,
Chestnut Hill,
Pennsylvania,
1964

Throughout the early 1960s, Venturi developed these themes of a broken domesticity, which distorted the sheltering and assertive nature of the home in favor of a playful delight in the orders and elements of architecture, in a number of buildings. He appropriated signs and decorative motifs, blew them up to a huge scale, and used them to festoon spaces that he squeezed together into puzzles of functional relations. Architecture and its certainties might have been under attack in the 1960s, but for Venturi the contradictions between order and daily life could open up a space of fun, allusion, and exploration. In *Complexity and Contradiction in Architecture*,[16] he argued that

"chaos is very near; its nearness, but its avoidance, gives . . . force."

The result was a very queer space that seemed to delight in its own artifice. The columns, grids, proportions, pediments, and sequences that architecture liked to decree in the world were still there, but they had become jumbled, blown up out of proportion and used in a way that contradicted their supposed purposes, leaving them as the elegant, but slightly askew, poses of a self-conscious order.

In later works, Venturi applied this same attitude toward public buildings and even town planning. Saying that "Main Street is almost alright,"[17] he delighted in the romance of small towns and the brash seductions of the commercial world. In an old-age home he designed in Philadelphia, a television antenna became a symbol for an electronic domesticity, while he designed a catalog store for the Best Company that was festooned with daisies, like a giant box of Kleenex tissues. Over time, his buildings became less queer. Together with his wife, Denise Scott Brown, he established a more rational and successful architectural practice, toning his outrageous elements down to the point where they could adorn hospitals, university buildings, and even the National Gallery in London. The work lost much of its force, only occasionally breaking out of its box with a column that was just much too large or in the middle of a path, a color whose pastel tint challenged good taste, or decorative flowers that refused to contain themselves to abstracted curls dancing around a cornice and instead started to cover the whole surface of a building.

Venturi's work at its best was outrageous. It brought a decorator's sensibility to the home and to the outside. The posing of historically familiar elements and emblems of domesticity, and then their denial by a change in scale, a juxtaposition, or a misuse, seemed to liberate these pieces to the point where they started to create another, much more unstable order around you. Similarly, decorative excess threatened to drown you in tendrils of a labyrinth of color and texture. The tight spaces that wound their way through these fragments of form then choreographed your activities into a dance of contradictions with no purpose other than a delight in the possibilities of making and using spaces. If Moore had proposed the domestic interior as a map of the self, Venturi redesigned that tracing of the geography of the everyday into rich costumes of ambiguity.

Figure 3.21
Venturi and
Scott Brown,
Best Catalog
Showroom,
Oxford Valley,
Pennsylvania,
1978

7

Together, Moore and Venturi created the parameters of what, at least in the United States, came to be known as postmodernism. Moore provided the sensual delights. He showed us that we could use modern technology and our knowledge of history to dissolve rigid forms into places where the body might bask in the sun, find a little piece of shelter, and dance through the different levels of daily life. It could bare itself to these delights, playing in a child's treasure chest or an opera of outrageous masks without worrying about the consequences. Venturi concentrated on designing the set and the toys themselves, giving us small icons of domesticity or belonging that you could play with and rearrange. Together, they deformed orders, made complex places in which you could trace a different life from the ones mandated by the closed boxes of traditional homes and offices. By making things and places that did not so much stop making sense as they challenged the senses to erect their own sense of order, they gave the inhabitant the chance to construct his or her own space.

Was there a sexual undercurrent in this work? Certainly the elements with which both Moore and Venturi were working had sexual undertones. In our society the home has always been associated with women and the orders of architecture with men. The postmodernists mixed and matched these elements. In doing so, they turned them both into self-conscious stage sets, as if you could erect your own sense of home and order, of femininity and masculinity (as our society defined them). Overblown and deformed phallic and womblike images abounded in the work. A delight in sensuality pervaded much of the work. I do not think that either architect set out to design a queer space, but the result was an architecture that certainly blew open the closet that contained the tricks of decoration and turned into a celebration of the body as it posed itself among the orders of appearance.

The energy of this work quickly disappeared into mainstream form-making. Even Moore's' and Venturi's later work sublimated much of the complexity and sensuality they originally displayed. The work was easy to copy, and postmodernism became a style that could liven up developer tracts, shopping malls, and office buildings everywhere. It did have a very useful function: it brought a sense of experience, of wit, and of a realization of the stage-set-like artifice that architecture uses to construct its orders in our society back to the forefront. For all of its problems, postmodern architecture made the massive bulks of glass, steel, and concrete more familiar, more responsive, and sometimes even more fun.

A small group of designers kept exploring along the pathways opened up by Venturi and Moore. They included several direct copyists, but also such architects as Robert A. M. Stern, who brought his own considerable historical knowledge to the game. A protégé of Philip Johnson, Stern most clearly set about queering modernism. His early work, such as the addition he designed for his own house in East Hampton in 1969 and the 1977 Lang House in rural Connecticut, was as thin and abstract as any modern environment, but literally bowed out with the force of the space inside. Baroque elements decorated the facades, and an almost Wildean yellow suffused the buildings. Stern's work was both more theatrical and thinner than that of the older generation, as if it were aspiring to a status of clothing. The certainties of architecture seemed to be disappearing into nothing but a magnificent and sometimes outrageous pose.

Figure 3.23
Robert A. M.
Stern,
Lang House,
Western
Connecticut,
1977

Stern also learned to tone his work down to fit the needs of straight clients, and went on to create some of the grandest and most correct mansions the East Coast has seen in this century. He began to work for the Disney Corporation (on whose board he sits), thus employing his talent for imaginative structures in the creation of theme parks. These seem to be the two paths of postmodernism: either to become the correct elaboration of architectural orders, reconciled with the comforts of interior decoration and its attention to the body and social relations; or to fly off into pure fantasyland,

where we are allowed to think of ourselves as fairies.

Yet the force of Moore's and Venturi's work continues to this era in the work of such inventive architects as Frank Israel. Self-consciously a pupil of both Moore and Venturi and openly queer, Israel delighted in deconstructing the very notions of domesticity. An early house design, the Clark House of 1980, proposed a pentagonal fortress as a refuge in the Hollywood Hills, while his interior designs of the late 1970s delighted in the use of pastel covers and multiple screens. As Israel matured, he developed his own formal language. It consisted of folded and bent plates that fused walls and ceilings into a kind of sheltering cloak that opened up in cracks where light spilled in. Moving under this sheltering form was a spiderweb of wood and sometimes steel lattices.

Israel did not break out of the familiar form of the ranch house. Even when he built a new form, as opposed to the extension of suburban homes that formed the core of his practice, he seemed to delight in bedrooms that were not sheltering abodes, but neutral boxes, living rooms that were split-level stages for a public version of family life, and kitchens that contained almost commercial eating booths. Notions of privacy and public appearance became confused, and then found an order in shrines for sex (over the beds) or entertainment (around the television sets). The Goldberg-Bean House, designed for a queer couple in 1992, pushed these themes to their furthest extreme, resulting in the dissolution of what had been a normal tract home into a colorful castle composed of aeries and aediculae, through which you flowed with all the ease modern open space planning and the loftlike living of a queer couple afforded.

An architect like Frank Israel realized the potential of a queer postmodernism. To him, the modern technology of glass and steel, but also of air-conditioning and electricity, could be liberating. It gave us open space and shelter without having to enclose us behind closed walls or under giant roofs. It served as the built equivalent of the changing attitudes toward one's sexuality: one could construct one's self in an open way. Privacy became something one chose and built, in relation to the masks of public appearance that one wore with as much grace as possible. The home became a place not to retreat, but to map the complex relations of the self to itself and to others through the markers that architecture provided. Like all good modernist architecture, the forms of the house were naked and revealing, so that the body could sense the materials, the connections, and the physical reality of the spatial enclosure instead of having to accept the orders the architect and society imposed on the act of building.

Figure 3.24
Frank Israel,
Bedroom,
Goldberg-Bean
House,
Los Angeles,
1992

137

Figure 3.25
Frank Israel,
Gillette Studio,
New York,
1986

The lessons of postmodernism, and of a queer architecture in general, are those of ambiguity and contradiction resolved through the body. The way that one constructs one's self in the real world can use the mediations and mirrors of architecture. By making spaces through which one can map one's relations and in which one can mirror one's self, one can find a place for one's self in the world. You realize that the orders of the world that might want to tell you what to do, what to make of yourself, how to appear, and what to be are filled with internal contradictions. This is mostly because they try to impose themselves on the vitality of lived experience and can never quite accomplish that task. Having come to this realization, you can treat them as masks or stage sets to use in your appearances. By providing a choreography of sensual delights, you can create your own relationship to the physical world. By decorating that world, you can create a technology of comfort that can form a buffer between you and the world, while creating another, fantasy-full environment that you can construct within the world. The queering of modernism into postmodernism and the reintegration of decoration and architecture has created spaces in which we can all build our own, private lives.

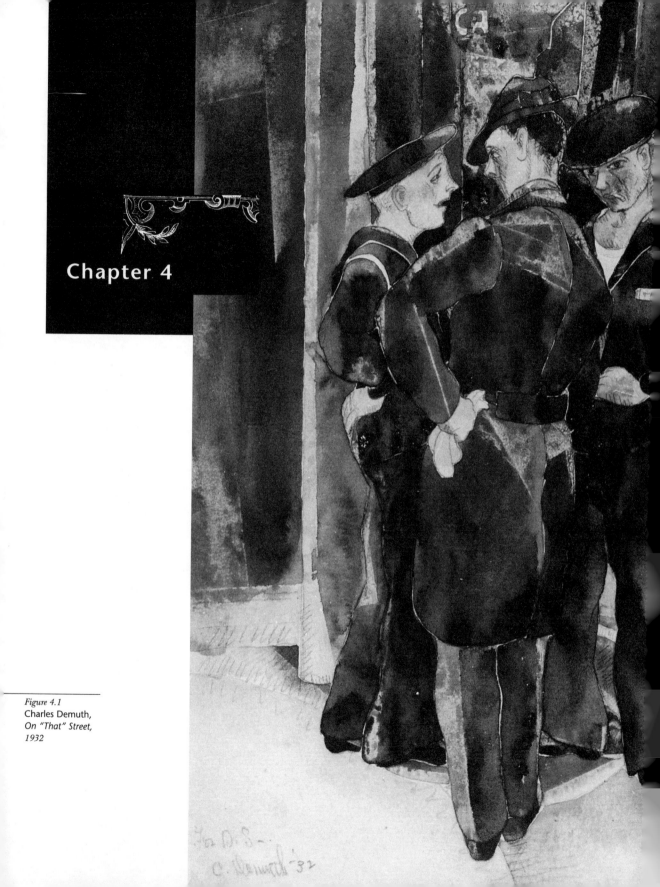

Chapter 4

Figure 4.1
Charles Demuth,
On "That" Street,
1932

From Cruising
to Community

1

For all of its colorful achievements, postmodernism has failed to achieve the same celebration of the liberating possibilities of modern life that it had found in the privacy of the home out in the public space of the city. Here queer spaces have provided another model for how we might queer the modernist urban environment into something more sensible, sensual, open, and self-constructive. This is the act of continual appropriation through cruising and the sexing of public spaces, but also through the building of functional neighborhoods for an emerging homosexual community.

The first queer spaces of the modern era were the dark alleys, unlit corners, and hidden rooms that queers found in the city itself. It was a space that could not be seen, had no contours, and never endured beyond the sexual act. Its order was and is that of gestures. What makes this space of cruising so important is that it shows that you don't have to make spaces to contain and encourage relations between people, because they will just appear exactly at the moment where they are least expected—or wanted. These spaces, moreover, have a sudden sensuality that belies the anonymous emptiness of the modern city.

Though the space of cruising is difficult to see, it has by now received enough attention and analysis, as well as description in evocative novels, that we can define its parts and pieces.[1] Its most fundamental characteristic is its ephemerality: it is a space that appears for a moment, then is gone, only to reappear when the circumstances are right. This queer space appears through an act of transformation that turns separation into its opposite, which is connection. Cruising is, as noted in Chapter 2, a fairly old activity that goes back at least as far as the seventeenth century. It is a network of routes queer men (and sometimes women) use as the physical expression of their community. It makes real a space that is essentially invisible, but that acts as a "counterspace" to the emerging transactional space of the middle-class city. Though centered on middle-class white men, it wipes out, at least for a moment, class distinctions just as surely as it allows the middle-class city to dissolve. This network of connections has a haunting quality Marcel Proust described:

. . . *forming a freemasonry far more extensive, more effective and less suspected that of the Lodges, for it rests upon an identity of tastes, needs, habits, dangers, apprenticeship, knowledge, traffic, vocabulary, and one in which even the members themselves, who intend not to know one another, recognize one another immediately by natural or conventional, involuntary or deliberate signs which indicate one of his kind to the beggar in the street in the person of the nobleman whose carriage door he is shutting, to the father in person of his daughter's suitor, to him who has sought healing, absolution, or legal defence in the doctor, the priest, or the barrister to whom he has had recourse; all of them obliged to protect their own secret but sharing with the others a secret which the rest of humanity does not suspect and which means to them the most wildly improbable tales of adventure seem true, for in this life of anachronistic fiction the ambassador is a bosom friend of the felon, the prince, with a certain insolent aplomb born of his aristocratic breeding which the timorous bourgeois lacks, on leaving the duchess's party goes off to confer in private with the ruffian;*

a reprobate section of the human collectivity, but an important part,
suspected where it does not exist, flaunting itself, insolent and immune,
where its existence is never guessed; numbering its adherents everywhere,
among the people, in the army, in the church, in prison, on the throne;
living, in short, at least to a great extent, in an affectionate and
perilous intimacy with the men of the other race, provoking them,
playing with them by speaking of its vice as of something alien to it . . .
applying to the object of their distraction, the same utilitarian instinct,
the same professional spirit which guides them in their career, they meet
these young men at gatherings to which no outsider is admitted any
more than to those that bring together collectors of old snuff-boxes,
Japanese prints or rare flowers, and at which, what with the pleasure
of gaining information, the practical value of making exchanges
and the fear of competition, there prevails simultaneously, as in
a stamp market, the close co-operation of specialists and the fierce
rivalries of the collectors.[2]

This invisible network spreads itself throughout the city, evidencing itself
only in gestures and certain isolated, emblematic items such as scarves or the colors
of one's clothes.[3] As many queers today still know, this network or "family" can let
you be at home in any city in the world. Once you have found the invisible thread,
it weaves together a tapestry of places that welcome you because of your sexual
preferences. This tissue includes stores, restaurants, bars, and even hotels that cater to
a queer community and surround the queer with spaces designed according to similar
principles or aesthetics. These spaces distinguish themselves by hiding in anonymity,
then exploding with richly decorated interiors. These interiors facilitate social
relations within the group by using mirrors and stages to allow the inhabitant to
display himself or herself, but also throw together queer people in social relations
that do not directly rely on sexual acts. This is the interior of a vast labyrinth
that by now crosses the boundaries not only of certain neighborhoods but of cities
and whole nations.

The nature of this space always remains sexual. It allows for cruising. At its most basic, cruising is an activity not unlike that of the aborigine "walkabout," in which the world becomes a score or script that one must bring alive by walking it.[4] Such celebrants of cruising as John Rechy talk of the cities they have cruised as such a world, where the self and society, the body and the body of the city and the pain and joy of this revelation merge:

Later I would think of America as one vast City of Night stretching gaudily from Times Square to Hollywood Boulevard—jukebox-winking, rock-n-roll-moaning: America at night fusing its darkcities into the unmistakable shape of loneliness.[5]

And I walked, that night, along the impassive nightlake—northward beyond the couples making love under the silhouetted trees. . . Along the dark lake. . . . And I looked back toward the magnificent Chicago skyline: that magic cyclorama embracing the water. Even the buildings which earlier seemed like giants marching snobbishly into the lake, now softened, blended into a glittering network of lights, lighted checkerboard. . . . And I know what it is I have searched beyond Neil's immediate world of sought pain— something momentarily lost—something found again in the park, the fugitive rooms, the derelict jungles; the world of uninvited, unasked-for pain. . . found now, liberatingly, even in the memory of Neil himself. And I could think in that moment, for the first time really: It's possible to hate the filthy world and still love it with an abstract pitying love.[6]

Figure 4.2a
The Ramble,
Central Park,
New York

The city of night is a place where the solid forms of everyday appearance do not so much disappear as they turn into ghosts. These more ephemeral apparitions serve to remind the cruiser of both their own restrictions and the bodies that find themselves lost in the urban grid. The cruising ground becomes a way of carefully tracing the contours of the city in all of its rational, functional reality, and inscribing one's self in that anonymous world. This is obviously not an altogether pleasant activity, as it involves an awareness of absence, pain, and loneliness, but it remains a validating one. The cruiser sings his world, however plaintively, alive.

It is also a world shot through with desire and fulfillment, where the passion of the moment becomes a repeated defense against the onslaught of the world. As the cruiser withdraws behind bushes or in a dark alley and makes himself vulnerable by dropping his pants or crouching in front of another man, he escapes, however momentarily.

Space and its constraints disappear in favor of the intimacy of sex,

one that participants often describe as overwhelming in its textures, smells, and sounds. It is as if they have been able to place a lens on the city, changing its scale to reveal another, much more material world that was always lurking right below the bland, everyday surfaces:

> As he moves into the periphery of the dusky cavern, he's aware of his bare feet touching the hot sand. He pauses, to feel the texture of the grains of crushed white earth. . . . Under the pier, the sand is moist.

*He passes from day to twilight to night in moments. In this darkness
only violence or sex can happen. An experienced hunter, Jim knows that
although he sees no one yet in the murky mist—and his eyes are
adjusting quickly—soon, very soon, figures will emerge. Shadows
within shadows. For moments, he stands in the twilit area; exhibiting
his body, making sure, as always, that he is clearly seen. Look. There's a
black solitary outline in the depths of the pier. Jim moves farther into the
shadowed world, The sand, untouched by the sun, becomes wetter. His
eyes adjust totally. Beyond, the tide rises. Swoosh! Swoosh. Swoosh!
Swoosh. Sounds echoing in the dark. Through slits left exposed by
boards fallen in diagonal patterns on the sand, shafts of light penetrate
like cold knives. . . . Two more outlines have materialized about Jim—
he feels more mouths. His mind explodes with outlaw images: men and
men and men, forbidden contacts, free, time crushed, intimate forbidden
strangers. Sensations increase, a tongue slides over his balls, another on
his ass, his cock still only simulating entry into the anxious asshole.
And now his lips are on those of a beautiful youngman suddenly beside
him, and in one swift thrust Jim's cock enters the grinding ass, and his
hand holds the squirting cock of the naked youngman he's fucking.
Male and male and male, hard limbs, hard cocks, hard muscles, hard
stomachs, strong bodies, male and male.*[7]

The space of cruising is thus one of escape into a material
reality. It finds the places in the city where such experiences are possible.
This usually means parks, the places we reserve as a respite from
urban reality within the city itself, or the cracks within the fabric itself,
such as dark alleys or unused buildings. Cruising grounds unerringly occur
at the places where the supposed rationale of the urban structure falls
apart because it is not functional. Cruising brings a new place back to life
either where we need to escape from our socially acceptable spaces
and places or where such places have come apart.

Figure 4.2b
Pier 52,
New York,
1977

Though the basic truth about the space of cruising is that it relies on the knowledge of the body rather than on analysis to work, this space does have certain definable characteristics. First, it needs conditions that in and of themselves dissolve walls and other constraints. This means that most cruising takes place either at night or inside dark, unused buildings. The latter include both abandoned structures and the empty, repetitive space of certain movie theaters. Second, such a space must be labyrinthine. It must frustrate "normal" use and detection by providing multiple barriers to intervention or observation. Cruising grounds include the "rambles" or self-consciously romantic byways of urban parks, or the spaces of alleys and cubicles inside unused buildings. Third, cruising finds the edges of both the city as a whole and buildings within the city. It exploits the points where truck drivers and other transient sailors of the postmodern sea gather, the places where the city breaks down into fields, and the stoops, porticos, windows, and doorways of buildings. Fourth, cruising grounds have to parallel, but not be the same as, the public spaces of the city. They are at the edges of Times Square or in the alleys that run alongside Santa Monica Boulevard or Melrose Avenue in Los Angeles.

In all of these ways, cruising grounds have an unerring way of finding the place where the city dissolves and sensuality can come to the fore. It makes you aware of your body and your surroundings as they merge in the queer act itself. This act takes place in silence, through a choreography of gestures that includes the movement of the car and can turn the space of the automobile, itself somewhere in between the contours of the body and a reflection of the rational orders of the city, into an actual place of action. The car, as both an instrument and a location, a lonely bubble and protected shelter, a physical implement and a moving vision, a mass-produced object and a personal space, might be the ultimate icon of cruising.

Cruising reveals an essential loneliness.

This is, however, a loneliness that is aware of its own space, rather than a mere separation. It is the continually reenacted search for connection, the revelation of anonymity in the most intimate knowledge of the space of the body, the darkness of the unused city, and the liveliness of disconnected orgasms that make Rechy's central condition so bittersweet. This is a loneliness that is the natural opposite of the walls of separation, fear, and distance that are meant to create community within their confines. By revealing the fallacy of such devices, cruising opens up the space of emptiness in the modern city and sings it alive through the actions of the queer body. It pushes the body and the city to the edge:

> *Of course, the ultimate backroom for the heaviest sleaze action—a backroom for the entire city, in fact—were the piers that lined the Hudson River: full of gaping holes to the river below, dangling gantries, and girdered catwalks, they were the very definition of dangerous and at night,* extremely *dark. . . . The action, when it happened, was* extreme, *as was the image. It was about stretching those very limits, reaching new highs, crossing new thresholds. Of intensity. Into the forbidden. Breaking more taboos.*[8]

2

Such moments of obscenity have, over the centuries, found their "natural theaters of action," as Edward Delph calls the tearooms and other places of assignation. These have eventually become spaces that queers specifically devote to such activities. Some of these spaces have embedded themselves in the social fabric of the city.[9]

Figure 4.3
Diagram of the
Ariston Bathhouse,
New York,
drawn by
a policeman
after a raid,
1903

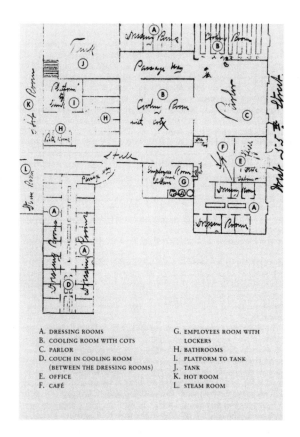

A. DRESSING ROOMS
B. COOLING ROOM WITH COTS
C. PARLOR
D. COUCH IN COOLING ROOM
   (BETWEEN THE DRESSING ROOMS)
E. OFFICE
F. CAFÉ

G. EMPLOYEES ROOM WITH
   LOCKERS
H. BATHROOMS
I. PLATFORM TO TANK
J. TANK
K. HOT ROOM
L. STEAM ROOM

The most famous example of a definable node of cruising is the tearoom or public bathroom in which sexual acts take place. Here the stalls that are supposed to provide privacy to a body that sees its reality as shameful become scrims. They allow for sexual connection at least in part because they screen out the social identity of the participants, allowing them to concentrate on the pleasure of the body. Urinals, on the other hand, are places where the public mask remains, but suddenly opens up through the appearance of the parts of the body that are usually most hidden, creating an eruption of sensuality in the aseptic, white environment of the tiled rest room.

The tearoom inscribes sex in a space that would usually imply its opposite by exploiting the one place where the spatial separation that guarantees "normal" social relations falls apart, namely when the masks of clothing, speech, and architecture that surround us have to open up to acknowledge the reality of our bodies.

It does so in a public space that in itself reveals the essence of all such supposedly noble environments: it is an amenity that makes visible the essentially infrastructural nature of the public realm. Instead of the empty plazas or café'd squares of the traditional city or even the tree-lined boulevards that we imagine as the essence of even the most gargantuan freeways, public rest rooms are places where the hidden network of pipes—the system of services that allows the urban agglomeration to work—becomes visible and serves a direct function. Tearooms occur in the bowels of courthouses and libraries and at rest stops, exploiting both the anonymity of such places, thus revealing the fact that "public" means that a space is characterless, and revealing the irreducible fact of bodily existence that is usually paved over, gridded, and hidden by such noble edifices.

The gridded white tiles and bare concrete of most of these spaces almost parody the ideals of modern architecture, which wanted to blot out the difference between interior and exterior, public and private, self and others, in favor of an abstract reality. Here sewage pipes and mirrors coexist in a world of white disinfectant, allowing the body to ironically stand out in greater contrast. The decay in our social services is itself mirrored in the inability to keep these places clean, so that real life seeps in through smells, graffiti, and other signs of use. What remains is the invisibility of the bodies, except when the sexual act erupts. The actors embed this performance in a careful choreography of gestures, activities, and roles that range from a lookout to a passive and an active participant to voyeurs. Observers who have tried to document this scene speak of it in terms of transactions and roles, as if this were a business activity, but one that has the body as its only capital and that results in the instant gratification of desire without any productive result.

Paradoxically, the tearoom seems to release its inhabitants from the everyday. Because they do not speak to each other, and because dress and position matter little compared to the size of one's member or one's age, the tearoom becomes one of the few public spaces that actually serve to liberate their inhabitants from the bounds of everyday existence. It is here that one usually finds "straight" men who only "occasionally" indulge in same-sex activities, whether because of their own or society's repressive structures or because they see this particular form of bonding as performing a particular function in a wider sexual menu. Here queerness erupts into the fabric of the everyday and erects an alternative web of connections out of "the craftsmanship in subtle connections."[10] The truck stop on the other hand, is a node in a vast network of continual connection, and is a place of escape for young queer men who find themselves bound to a certain place.[11] These are places where transient sex creates a moment of connection. To some, they become encampments where men can find the most basic notions of shelter without the constraints the city has layered on such form. They are also at the edge of civilization, places where things fall apart or decay:

Homes that move, dens that can be closed off, in the middle of the city. The older lorries have slightly rusted, chrome-plated door handles. I want quietly to press a handle down, to climb in. Closed, these cabins, as sometimes are the other temporary dens of this city, the builders' huts, the canvas and metal meshed tents of gas, electricity and telecom men. Huts, tents, dens: always loved them.[12]

Figure 4.4
Gymnasium,
San Francisco,
1996

Gymnasia or sports clubs are altogether different queer spaces. Here the act of cruising becomes internalized around the circuit of the weight machines, where the body mirrors itself in a space where boundaries disappear. Here the queer man is both flaneur and object of desire, working in a parody of work, torturing his body without hurting it.[13] These spaces are all about the body displaying itself in the process of becoming its ideal.

Architecture disappears into glass and machines. Gyms represent a vernacular version of the modernist utopia, where reality fades away into reflections. Queer men cruise these spaces, displaying themselves and watching others, while only slightly sublimating their desire into the repetitive motion of machines. In queer communities such as West Hollywood, the gym is the largest building in the neighborhood, a monument to the cruising grounds that built the first queer-controlled city in the country. Expanses of picture windows display the action and allow for panoramic views of that city. The walls of architecture dissolve to allow the cruiser to view the body and the body to feel liberated in his view of the city.

Cruising has found its free space.

Sexual activity does (or did) sometimes take place in the gyms, though it was usually confined to the showers and steam rooms in the more private parts of the buildings. Even in public gyms such activities take place. Most notable as cruising grounds are the gyms of public schools and universities. Cruising has a home at the heart of these middle-class men's houses, where they are most concentrated on building new, male bodies. There is a notorious sequence at the University of California at Berkeley gym. After passing through security, the queer man can find a moment of voyeurism in a small café that lets him look through a picture window at the water polo team's practice platform. Then he can go down to the locker rooms.

Figure 4.5
Paul Cadmus,
*Y.M.C.A. Locker
Room,
1933*

Upon entering this space, he finds himself on axis with the showers. Men are standing around poles in the middle of the room, rather than the sides, and are backlit by clerestory windows. The viewer is treated to a gauzy display of male nudes. After he walks past the endless grid of lockers, getting glimpses of undressing or dressing men, sheds his own clothes, and participates in the world of the shower, the queer man can get one last glimpse by drying his hair along a wall that sports dryers placed so that you must stand facing the showers. Nobody knows whether this sequence was deliberately designed to embed cruising within this august academic institution, but the effect is unmistakable and much exploited by local queers.[14]

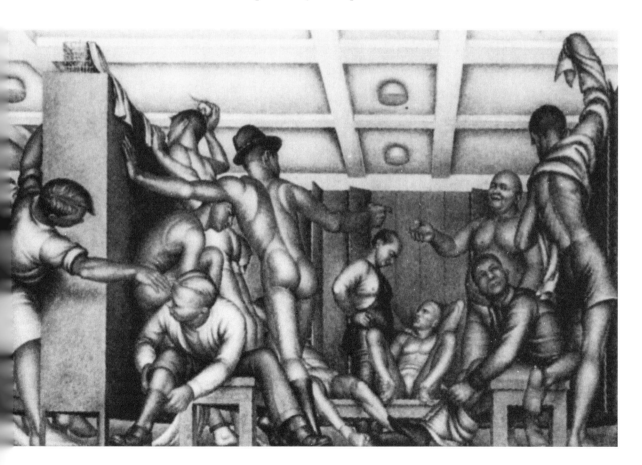

3

It is not always enough to have this invisible fabric weaving together spaces. Over the years, queers have built institutions that formalize the world of cruising in an overt manner. In the bars, dance halls, baths, and sex clubs of the queer culture you can find an attempt to turn the ephemeral world of cruising into something more durable and identifiable. In doing so, queers create monuments to an emerging queer community, but also threaten to lose the lonely beauty of such spaces into something much more commercial, useful, and thus rather limiting.

Queer spaces of meeting and assignation emerged in the seventeenth century as "molly houses" or other places where sex was available for sale. They became gathering places for queer men and thus points where the community became visible. Periodic raids on such places defined the queer community by the company it kept. The space of a queer community became a place of gaudy pleasures contained within an anonymous facade, as if it were a more intense version of the brothel that served as the obscene counter to the emerging norms of social behavior and its highly visible, rational scenes.

By the end of the nineteenth century, queer dance halls and bars began to take on a life of their own. They developed their own characteristic contours. In many ways, they mirrored the cruising grounds. Early bars depended heavily on barriers and labyrinthine spaces, darkness and a position on the edge of town. For middle-class men, the latter position meant a location at the point where their order broke down: in the slums.[15] Here class barriers fell and morality disappeared in a mirrored, heavily compartmentalized environment. In the twentieth century, the gay space split: some bars and places of gathering started more and more to mirror the entertainment worlds of a straight culture, and disappeared into the appropriation of space for certain times or occasions. Others became more and more extreme in their isolation, separation, and distinct characteristics.

George Chauncey has traced the emergence of gay bars in the twentieth century in New York, noting that the early queer gathering spaces were open. They offered their entertainment to all comers. The gay bars, dance halls, and restaurants were places of intense celebration and exuberant appearances. Here men and women dressed in parodies of the standard models of high fashion, often of the opposite sex, turning these places into celebrations of the height of artifice. The Harlem Balls, where African-American men appeared in drag, generated a whole genre of theater. They were among the most intense visual moments in the New York landscape. Here the group that found itself doubly outcast, as both black and queer, created the most outrageous queering of high society center.[16]

Even on a smaller, less outrageous scale, this theatricality *points to one of the central strategies deployed by gay men for claiming space in the city. They regularly sought to emphasize the theatricality of everyday interactions and to use their style to turn The Life and other locales into the equivalent of a stage, where their flouting of gender conventions seemed less objectionable because it was less threatening.*[17]

The public equivalent of the private exaggeration of grand styles made the city come alive with a pageant of colors, clothes, and gestures. Here the intensity of urban culture bore strange fruit, freeing a space of intense experience within the most anonymous settings.

After the Second World War, when the military broke down many barriers and, for a while, threw together men of all classes and sexual preferences, urban authorities began to clamp down on such free-flowing institutionalized parties, forcing queer gathering spaces to go back underground. The model now became the speakeasy, rather than the café of flaneurs. A queer life could still flourish, but it had to do so often literally underground, out of sight and out of reach for most of the straight population.

Over time, this model solidified into a standard appearance for queer bars all across the country. Urban geographers have by now documented the type with a great deal of precision.[18] Queer bars revel in anonymous structures, often on the outskirts of what are considered acceptable neighborhoods, but near good transportation and work. This means that they have gathered at the edges of downtown areas and have become the magnets for development of dilapidated areas. Gay bars have occupied the meat-packing district of the West Village in New York, the anonymous, leftover strip of Santa Monica Boulevard in Los Angeles, and the warehouses of the South of Market area in San Francisco, attracting attention, patrons, and eventually other businesses to such areas. They have used the voids of the city and filled them with life.

Figure 4.6
West Street,
New York,
1977

The only thing that distinguished many gay bars until the 1970s (and still sets them apart from straight gathering places in many small towns) was a sign that announced a name. The only way queer men often know to go into such a space is through an invisible spatial network, that of rumor and hearsay, which is sometimes codified in gay travel guides. The entrance is often in the rear, to allow a greater degree of anonymity. The queer bar wears a mask that only fellow wearers can read.

Once inside, the queer bar has most of the same ingredients as its straight equivalent, except that they are, once again, exaggerated. Mirrors abound, so that customers can reflect themselves and engage others without direct contact. There is also plenty of "runway space," long strips of empty territory, sometimes even raised, where men can display themselves to a line of spectators. The social ritual of display and desire here has a stage set with a forthrightness that often startles the uninitiated.

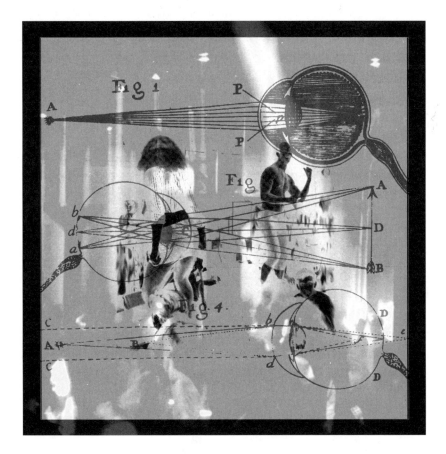

Figure 4.7
Steve Jaycox,
An Anonymous
Gay Bar Interior,
1996

During the 1970s, what had been vestigial dance floors flourished into the main attraction of most queer bars. Queers picked up on the transformation of music from the expression of the skill of the musician to the programmed rhythms of a machine orchestrated by performers wearing masks. Disco became the queer house music, and its forms were as ahuman as the sounds: multiple colored lights, strobes, and mirrored surfaces dissolved space, made bodies seemingly discontinuous, and exaggerated appearances. The disco picked up on the theatrical light shows that had come out of the "trips festivals" and rock concerts of the 1960s and mass-produced them into programmed moments of letting go of one's body, normalcy, and all connections to material reality. Only rhythm and flashes of images mattered. Occasionally a spotlight would pick out one particular body as an object of display, or go-go boys would act out the idealized version of the queer body in motion.

The space of the disco was one of the most radical environments Western society has created in the last fifty years. More and more technology was brought to bear on the creation of an environment that had no bounds, no solidity, and no reality. The lights, mirrors, and sounds acted together to create such a degree of disorientation that, even without the aid of drugs or orgasm, the world dissolved. The DJs, lighting experts, and set designers (most of them anonymous)[19] who designed these spaces replaced reality with pure rhythm and pulses of light, which were mechanized versions of the sexual act, but also of the heartbeat that is usually hidden inside the body. Once stripped down to a mechanical rhythm with no form, it then reconstructed the body, often stripped down to very few clothes and buffed up by hours at the gym. The queer man could dance himself alive in space in a continuous performance that created a community of such appearances. This was a place of seeming freedom, liberated by the technology of light and music.

The Saint, one of the most expensive and elaborate discos in New York, represented the type. Located on the margins of the Village on a rather rough stretch of street, the building presented nothing but black doors to the outside world. Past the entrance you found steel-mesh frames that contained the coat check. Here you shed your street identity in almost complete darkness. After this ritual preparation, you headed up one of two ramps framing a completely empty space. Ghosts of figures moved past, touching, feeling, and posing. Moving through the void, you became aware of the music in a far-off place above you. Finally, you arrived at your destination: a geodesic dome of translucent fabric. This was both a dance floor and a planetarium, a globe that summed up an abstracted world where everything, including straight walls, disappeared in a mosaic of continually changing rhythms of light and sound.

Beyond the dome, in the nether reaches of this vast structure, was only darkness. Here men gathered for assignations and drugs, escaping even further from reality.

4

By the 1980s, the gay bar had retreated from reality about as far as you could go. Smaller bars pushed reality far away in other ways. Role-playing became so diversified that certain bars accepted only patrons dressed as cowboys or policemen: they had turned their interiors into make-believe versions of popular myths. Sex itself became more and more important in such spaces, as if the hidden, obscene moments were erupting out into the scene. Outrageous displays of sexual role-playing, including men harnessed in the middle of the room as sexual objects and tanks for "water sports," dissolved the bounds of propriety completely.

An extreme space, one in which the self turned into only a
node of sexual activity wearing a mask of a particular obsession,
took over. Edmund White described a poignant version he
encountered in the West Village:

> After a while we drifted into the back room, which was so dark I never
> received a sense of its dimensions, though I do remember standing on a
> platform and staring through the slowly revolving blades of a fan into a
> cubbyhole where one naked man was fucking another. A flickering
> candle illuminated them. It was never clear whether they were customers
> or hired entertainment; the fan did give them the look of actors in a
> silent movie.[20]

The logical extreme of such spaces was the sex
club. The precedents for such a monofunctional environment
go back at least to the turn of the century, when queer men
began using Turkish baths and other places of cleansing that
catered to an immigrant, working-class community as places of
assignation. They were oases of sensuality where the body could
strip itself of all outside appearances to enjoy itself in an environment dissolving into water and steam. The baths kept alive
the delights of the Roman bath, and for immigrants were places
of simple hygiene and community-building. Upper-or middle-
class men began using them as an escape from their own lives,
finding here a sensuality in communal gathering that had no
place in the rational world of middle-class work or living.[21]

By the 1930s, queer baths had established themselves as places
of assignation and sometimes even community-building, as Chauncey
deduces from memoirs and police records of the period. Like the bars, the
baths had a period of flowering, and then were forced to become ever
more anonymous and inward-turned, before erupting in a final spurt of
exuberance in the 1970s and early 1980s. Like bars, these baths established
a standardized organization that was, however, much more elaborate than
the simple runways and mirrors of the bar.[22]

The baths shared a gated entrance, but the act of shedding your social mask and revealing yourself was much more ritualized in the locker rooms. Wearing little if anything, you would then enter into a circuit of space. Here you would find a sensual abstraction of the spaces of the city. There were gathering spaces of abstract design, mainly in the steam rooms, where large groups of men could engage in a communal activity—namely sex. The gridded tiles that surrounded these rooms, the semidarkness, and the emptiness of expanses of water parodied the squares of middle-class gathering.

Figure 4.8
Charles Demuth,
A Turkish Bath,
1916

Internal boulevards of flaneurs, where men would cruise by each other as they looked for the wares they wished to consume, connected these spaces. In another perversion, these consumables were other men, who displayed themselves in small cubicles whose doors they left open. Sometimes you were invited only to watch, other times to obtain the object of desire, or even to become an object of sexual use yourself. The barriers between subject and object, what you could own and what you were, broke down in continual dramas of connection, fulfillment, and then abandonment.

Separate from these open rooms were the little cubicles or lockers where you could store your belongings and then stay. You would be naked, but protected in a miniature of your private house. There you could create more private (sexual) relations, occasionally inviting a few others to join you. These little bedrooms became the most irreducible abstraction of home within this miniature city of desire. They were places where there was only your body and the sexual act.

Finally, there were places of respite within the sexual city. These were lounges where men could gather to watch television, eat and drink, or even sleep. Like public parks or living rooms, they were places of leisure where the gridded walls and repetitive spatial order broke down into something less formal, more flowing, and halfway between public and private space. It was these spaces that many queers described as giving them a sense of community, while liberating them in a mist of steam that liberated them from physical constraints.[23]

After the AIDS epidemic had closed down most bathhouses and discos in the 1980s, a new type emerged. This was the sex club pure and simple, where all the activities of cruising were simplified. These were even more ephemeral spaces, ones that sometimes even took place in bars or living rooms and existed only as the momentary node in an invisible network established through friendships, advertisements, and rumor. Here men would gather for sex and sex only, usually with men like them.

Figure 4.9
Steve Jaycox,
Sex Club Interior,
1996

The complexity of previous queer spaces, including their elaborate parodies of the straight world and their mixing of different kinds of men, here dissolved into nothing but barns where young, fit men could mirror themselves before attempting to make their experience of self in space real through sex. A recent example in San Francisco took this spatial order to a logical extreme by setting out a grid of tents in a loftlike space, as if re-creating the mining camps that were the foundation of much of Northern California's culture in all of its ephemerality and male-only isolation.

Henry Urbach has documented one such club, pointing out its most salient features. Central to its operation were both its anonymity and its labyrinthine interior, so that a completely disconnected space appeared.

Here watching became everything:

instead of the semidark of steam rooms or the implications of the runway, men could sit on bleachers, watching the action while opening themselves up to obscene observation from below. The rooms had no ceilings and were only notional retreats. The cruising circuit always turned back on itself:

Exit the labyrinth at the rear and move along the brick wall painted white. Peer through windows fitted with metal bars into the narrow space behind; find the passageway at the far corner and traverse the alley along its length, past the metal platform, toward the dark corner where they are waiting. Come out again and move around to the other side of the labyrinth. Huddle beneath the stairs with dozens of others. Rub against the walls; rub against the bodies. Upstairs, pass through another lounge—sofa and chairs, a glass bowl of condoms, a cloud of cigarette smoke. Find the bleachers at the far edge of the lounge.
Note how the vertical spacing of bleacher risers position mouths and genitals for each coupling. Observe that the bleachers situate spectators as participants, participants as spectacle. Move further along to a balcony where a screened aperture frames a view into the labyrinth of cells below. Survey the scene, peer into the booths, watch those who watch; share others' intimacy. Recall the prisoner expecting a guard, the confessor awaiting a priest; wait here, trembling, for a redemptive other, for a release from longing and absence. Wait here for an anonymous angel. In the sex club, architecture and bodies converge. Rubbing, piercing, probing: these activities are enacted at once spatially and sexually, with walls as with flesh. Bodies crowd into corners, into chamber and doorways, under stairs—intensifying the erotic encounter by pressing up against spatial boundaries.[24]

Parodies and abstractions of social space become so stylized as to lose all connection with the outside world, so that the sex club becomes a container of "homoerotic spaces without their homophobic other."[25] For Urbach, this is an important moment in queer space, as it allows queers to create "fortresses" of self-definition against the straight world. Ironically, it is the interpenetration of these two worlds that gives the sex club its raw energy:

> *As architecture and bodies converge, the urban exterior penetrates the club as well. Gritty walls, sticky floors, ripped upholstery, cracked fixtures: interior surfaces reiterate the tough materiality of the city beyond (as does the paradigmatic queer look, i.e., tattoos, piercings, ripped jeans, work boots). The multiplicity of interior spaces also recalls, in condensed form, the heterogeneous spatiality of the city at large— and invites the same kind of nomadic, itinerant flow on a different scale. Circulation within the club is a continuous process of local territorialization and deterritorialization as bodies coalesce, move apart, and regroup to optimize erotic practice. In addition to its urban ambiance, the sex club further brings the city within its interior by reframing a variety of elements from the landscape of homoerotic desire. The charged spaces of locker rooms, bleachers, and saunas, public bathrooms, sidewalks, and alleyways: these spatial tropes re-emerge inside the club to refer to, and reinvent, a half-real, half-imaginary landscape beyond.[26]*

This is the apotheosis of an urban queer space, one that frees the queer body into a realization of itself in the real world. The appropriation of space through cruising, the celebration of urban theater, the creation of moments of intense intimacy within the city, and the opening up of a space where the body can mirror itself and complete itself in an orgasmic moment and place of loss all create this queer world. Unfortunately, it is also a world of death.

5

The alternative to such spaces of negation is formed by the communities queer men and women have built out of cruising grounds. Instead of only using their invisible networks as routes between places of assignations, queers have also formalized them into real spaces where they can lead every aspect of their lives in an overt manner. Both ghettos and permeable neighborhoods, such enclaves have flourished in almost every major city in the Western world. The effect of their establishment has reached far beyond the queer community: they have become models, both positive and negative, for the redevelopment of the American city.[27]

At the core of queer community-building is the notion of "gentrification." The very word implies that a wealthy class is making its own space, and in many cases this is exactly what the "gay invasion" has been: the occupation of working-class or industrial areas by middle-class white men. They brought with them a set of ideas about how space should be used that, however, mimicked at least what they understood to be the older uses of these sections of the city.

As it became more acceptable to be queer in the decades after the Stonewall riots, the queer community developed its own normative standards and identity, and with it enough cohesion to establish itself in place. Queers were, however, not interested in imposing new, abstract spaces, as a previous generation of planners and urban pioneers had been, nor were they interested in creating anti-urban suburbs. They wanted to bring the city back to life, because it was only there that they could lead their lives. They wanted to create neighborhoods for themselves, where they could make a community. The group of people that, because of the way our society describes family structures and zones the relation between work, play, and living, had become most divorced from the notion of a communal experience of urban space had the most need to re-create it as everybody else was abandoning it.

The genesis of this space was a regularization of cruising grounds one observer has classified as the "Circuit":

> *The social networks included "cliques" and "crowds." Cliques functioned as friendship circles and met the men's basic social, emotional, and material needs. In this sense, they were surrogate families. A crowd consisted of a group of cliques that frequented the same meeting spot. . . . The crowds mixed in a round of meeting spots that was known as the "Circuit." The gathering places in the Circuit were mainly locales for social, recreational, or sexual activities. For example, the men dined in Circuit restaurants, worked out in Circuit gyms, cruised in Circuit bars, and had sex in Circuit bathhouses. In addition, the men attended Circuit meeting spots according to a fixed schedule called "Circuit hours."* [28]

This circuit made the desire for sameness into a social phenomenon by specifying the subgroups within the queer community. The central group that held the Circuit together was that of the "clones": middle-class men who dressed in extremely similar, almost uniform ways. With their closely cropped hair, their small mustaches, and their muscular but not bulky bodies, they were almost abstractions of the middle-class, middle-aged white male.

San Francisco was the place where the phenomenon of queer gentrification was most striking. Frances FitzGerald, in her book on the continuity of utopian ideals within a modern context, traces the development of a queer community that shifted from the anonymous nodes around gay bars to the residential communities farther from the center of downtown:

> Folsom Street was a night town—the Valley of the Kings, it was called, as opposed to the Valley of the Queens in the Tenderloin and the Valley of the Dolls on Polk Street. But in addition to the leather bars, a variety of gay restaurants, discotheques, bathhouses, and sex clubs had moved into its abandoned warehouses and manufacturing lofts. It was an entertainment place, and few people lived there. The Castro, by contrast, was a neighborhood. Though first settled by gays—homesteaded, as it were—in the early seventies, it was now the fulcrum of gay life. At first glance it was much like other neighborhoods: a four-block main street with a drugstore, corner groceries, a liquor store, dry cleaners, and a revival movie house whose facade had seen better days. . . . The main street ran off into quiet streets of two and three-story white-shingle houses. . . . In fact the neighborhood was like other neighborhoods except that on Saturdays and Sundays you could walk for blocks and see only young men dressed as it were for a hiking expedition. Also, the bookstore was a gay bookstore, the health club was a gay health club; and behind the shingles hung out on the street there was a gay real-estate brokerage, a gay lawyer's office, and the office of a gay psychiatrist. The bars were, with one exception, gay bars, and one of them, the Twin Peaks bar near Market Street, was, so Armistead told me, the first gay bar in the country to have picture windows on the street.[29]

The Castro was the first queer public space.

At its height, it was a gay Disneyland version of a normal neighborhood, with Castro serving as its Main Street and the bars serving as the rides. It looked like a normal neighborhood, but something was slightly off: the houses were too clean, too colorful, and too intensely occupied. Where in the rest of the country street life had disappeared, in the Castro it became so intense as to turn into a mob during a sunny weekend. As queer middle-class men pushed out different classes and ethnic groups, it also became increasingly homogeneous. It was the queer "City on the Hill," here turned into a valley that delighted in its ability to create a pure pleasure zone.[30]

Figure 4.10
Map of Gay
Residential Areas
in San Francisco,
1977

There was a particular aesthetic to such places. Manuel Castells, in his groundbreaking study of the Castro, attributes this style to the classic "third sex" position of queer American men:

> . . . *the artistic talents of many gays have accounted for one of the most beautiful urban renovations known in American cities. The effects on urban aesthetics have gone beyond the careful painting of the original Victorian facades. Apart from the impressive interior decoration of the imaginatively remodeled flats the impact can be seen in the well-designed treatment of semi-public spaces—between the front door and the pavement for example; in all, a very unusual architectural improvement in the highly individualistic world of American cities. . . . There is, in fact, a theoretical social explanation for such a talent. Gay men are in the midst of two processes of socialization, each one leading to a specific set of values. On the one hand, they grow up as men, and therefore are taught to believe in the values of power, conquest, and self-affirmation, values that in American society tend to be expressed through money or, in other words, through the dominance of exchange value. At the same time, because of the feelings that many have had to hide for years, and some for their entire life, they develop a special sensitiveness, a desire for communication, a high esteem of solidarity and tenderness that brings them closer to women's culture.*

This is not, however, because gays are "feminine," but, like women, their oppression and discrimination creates a distance from the values of conquest and domination which they are supposed to share as men. Thus, they tend to consider the use value of their personal lives as important, or worth more than the exchange value that could be acquired without ever obtaining the greatest reward of all—to be themselves. And yet power and money still matter for many gay men. The spatial expression of this twofold desire for exchange value and use value is, in our opinion, housing renovation. On the one hand they occupy a building, and make it distinctive and valuable. On the other hand, there is something else going on in the restored building: it has beauty, comfort, and sensuality, and is saying something to the city while expressing something to its own dwellers. And when a space becomes meaningful, exchange value is no longer the dominant issue. This is perhaps the most important contribution of the gay community to the city: not only housing improvement but urban meaningfulness.[31]

Queers, who only a short while before had been able to construct a social identity only as painted ladies, now were busy resurrecting the Painted Ladies of San Francisco, turning them into masks for their newly domestic lives. Whether this decorative impulse came from their sensitivity to issues our society has assigned to the female realm, or whether they were merely interested in making themselves at home in the city by appropriating its historic forms, the result was an exuberant celebration of the colorful chaos that made up the modernizing city of the late nineteenth and early twentieth century, when you could still believe that the city held promise for the future. Queers were building, in image if not in fact, not a perfect place, but the act of constructing such a place.

That idea of continual (self-)reconstruction extended into the appropriation of public space. Many observers have pointed out that the gay community developed around festivals such as the Halloween and Gay Pride parades, which were themselves no more than larger versions of the "Circuit." Unlike neighborhoods that kept themselves together by acting out the rituals of family based around church and playground, or that offered integrated places to work, shop, and live, queer communities such as the Castro made themselves real by continually reenacting the very idea of community as a place where people come together to create social connections. That these connections had a sexual base made them only more real, and that they resulted in an exuberant display of sameness strengthened them. The self-conscious construction of a queer space as the continual reconstruction of the self in and as the city was perhaps the most important and certainly the most visible contribution queers have made to the American city.

It is worth pointing out the continuity between such reconstructions and the hippie movement that had made San Francisco its capital during the late 1960s. As Castells points out,[32] queers learned the whole idea of reinhabiting the city from the hippies, and also copied the notion of communal living from them. It was also the hippies, I would contend, who kept alive the Arts and Crafts ideals of creating a better world through the revelation of material and structure in the making of the objects and spaces of everyday life. The hippies had pioneered, finally, the very notion that one can create what has by now come to be known as a "lifestyle": the formalization of value systems, methods of behavior, and ways of presenting one's self that evidences itself in everything from clothing to the car one drives, and has its most stable reference point in where one lives and how one uses those spaces. The queer space of the city was the quintessential lifestyle place.

Just as the gay flaneur of the Wildean years had been the essence of the self-conscious middle-class man who had to make a new world for himself, so the gay clone was at the vanguard of the transformation of the sixties revolutions into the more stable consumerist structures of the 1980s yuppies. The clone was the proto-yuppie, and neighborhoods such as the Castro and Greenwich Village were his space:

> *Greenwich Village isn't a symbolic place for me anymore, a kind of rive gauche Gotham where suburban kids go to take guitar lessons.*

It's real now, a place where unimaginative people come to sin.

Figure 4.11
Gay Pride Parade,
San Francisco,
1996

It has broken water pipes, noisy heterosexual neighbors, obnoxious tourists, homeless panhandlers. But it's a place where the neighborhood drunks know you by name and wave as you walk home from another insane day at work or a night at the Philharmonic or a hotel roll in the hay with a dazzling new boy from the Gaiety, or a dinner with a dozen sober gay and lesbian poet friends. . . . It's a place where dogs know each other's trees, where you can see the Empire State Building, the Chrysler building, the World Trade Center, the Hudson River, and the Macy's Fourth-of-July fireworks from your own tarry roof, or sit on the stoop and watch the New Kids on the Block catapult from a pair of limos into the Pink Tea Cup, the local soul-food diner across the street. It's a place where "hometown" seems like a reality, a place immune to nothing, a city place with all its organs intact, all its juices flowing, and all its emotions available for use. . . . [33]

6

The place of women in these areas is controversial. Certainly concentrations of lesbian women began to appear almost immediately after and adjacent to queer male communities. These neighborhoods were considerably less visible. To a certain extent this is due, as Castells already pointed out, to the fact that women still have less money and power in our society, and thus do not have the resources to establish themselves. Castells' more controversial point is that women felt less of a need to create a communal place:

Women have rarely had these territorial aspirations: their world attaches more importance to relationships and their networks are ones of solidarity and affection. In this gay men behave first and foremost as men and lesbians as women. So when gay men try to liberate themselves from cultural and sexual oppression, they need a physical space from which to strike out. Lesbians on the other hand tend to create their own rich, inner world and political relationship with higher, societal levels. They are "placeless" and much more radical in their struggle.[34]

Several women have objected to such descriptions,[35] pointing to the creation of such strong lesbian neighborhoods as the Mission in San Francisco and Park Slope in New York,[36] yet such neighborhoods lack the outward appearance that makes them cohere as visible spaces in areas dominated by men. This is not necessarily a bad thing. Lesbian communities have tended to be stronger, longer-lasting, and less exclusive, so that they point the way toward the making of a realized social sphere that does not repeat the ghettolike isolation in which gay men have found themselves. Instead, lesbian communities have tended to be more flexible, but perhaps also more pervasive:

> *The very concentration of lesbians has created a recognizable social space—recognizable most importantly to each other, but increasingly the "straight" population as well. The concentration can be attributed in large part to lesbian social networking, the success of which has contributed to the neighborhood's continuing gentrification, and consequently, to lesbian displacement. The social networking process and its spatial ramifications remind me of an early 1980s TV shampoo commercial. A woman's talking head fills the screen, saying that she liked the product so much: "I told two friends, and she told two friends. . . " Like images of reproducing cells, squares of women's faces fill the screen, doubling in number and doubling again, until the screen is crowded with smiling women's faces.[37]*

This cellular tissue pervading neighborhoods makes it hard to describe or find, but perhaps also a better model for the making of a community in a society that organizes itself around cars and telecommunications. Increasingly, gay communities of both sexes have tended to atomize, turning into bulletin boards on the World Wide Web and circuits between isolated nodes in exurban locations.[38] This is perhaps a natural result of the growth of a self-consciously queer community. Like the immigrants who occupied near-inner-city neighborhoods before them, queers began by expanding from Silver Lake to West Hollywood, from the Castro to Noe Valley and Twin Peaks, and from the West Village to the East Village and Chelsea, before disappearing into far-flung neighborhoods across large urban agglomerations. There are now small queer pockets all over most American cities, but few of them have the coherence of the Castro. Again, women led the way, establishing the first exurban retreats and communities at the very edge of the city.[39]

7

What has been lost in this process has been a certain amount of political vision. At the height of its development, the Castro was perhaps the most vibrant urban center in San Francisco. It helped elect a mayor and dominated many political debates. Queers based there led the fight against the rapid expansion of the central business district and imposed their admittedly middle-class-male values for the development of the city on the rest of the community through zoning regulations and even a "beauty commission" that established laws for the design of skyscrapers. By heading an alliance of old neighborhood groups and other "marginal" forces such as African-Americans, queers promised to queer the whole American city into a pretty, open-ended, exuberant place, a continual retracing and reconstruction of the very notion of a civilized, bourgeois space.

Queer space could have been the whole American city.

Then the AIDS epidemic hit, and the fantastical structure of queer space as communal reconstruction disappeared, leaving the Castro and its kin as queer shopping arcades filled with the ghosts of their former exuberance.

Chapter 5

The Void and Other
Queer Spaces

1

The devastation the AIDS epidemic let loose on the queer community destroyed many of the spaces queers had created for themselves over the last century. The place of bodily pleasure, where the self could mirror itself in the other with every sense and celebrate the community of flesh; the tracing of the forgotten contours of the city through cruising; the electronic space of dancing and festive revelry; the comfortable and highly posed places of belonging queers had carved out within the rigid structures of the city and the ironic appropriation of its forms to create stage sets on which one could act out an artificial life—this whole city of forms became hollowed out by death and disease. I am reminded of nothing so much as Huizinga's *The Waning of the Middle Ages,* in which he describes a society whose rich culture of minstrel spaces, pilgrimages, and fairs became deserted before the Renaissance reoccupied the resulting voids with its rational structures.[1]

Out of this very void came a new queer space,

one that I can only describe as a queering of queerness: an attempt not so much to create a queer space as to reveal that space to us as queers, so that we could build an identity that would then be separate from real spaces of connection and community.

Being queer became a question of propaganda, consciously outrageous behavior, and examination of one's own (real or imagined) life. Though these spaces of mirroring are important, it is important to point out that they resulted in mirroring the self only as a constructed identity, not as a real person. Queerness became something you made, not something you lived. The sense that same-sex love was the basis of a certain identity could not survive a situation in which it was the very act of lovemaking that could destroy you. Perhaps Michel Foucault realized this when he opened himself up to the disease in the de Sadean bowels of San Francisco.[2]

AIDS destroyed queer space.

It did so not only literally, but also by making us aware of the self-destructive nature of the very notion of artifice. Perhaps nobody has described this realization better than the San Francisco writer Richard Rodriguez. To Rodriguez, the particular construction of queerness had its roots in the act of coming out, but that process revealed not just a joyous new chrysalis, but the revealing of mortality itself:

> To grow up homosexual is to live with secrets and within secrets. In no other place are those secrets more closely guarded than within the family home. The grammar of gay city borrows metaphors from the nineteenth-century house. "Coming out of the closet" is predicated upon family laundry, dirty linen, skeletons.[3]

Queerness reveals the home not just as the building block of a society and a city, but as a place where the body remains hidden and identity is subsumed into social relations. You are a brother, sister, or parent, and you must appear as a productive part of a family unit within an assigned space that exists at a remove from any real production. In this middle ground, the body and the self both disappear. By coming out, they are revealed, and they are not always pretty. It is for this reason, says Rodriguez, that queers are so obsessed with both body building and decorating.

They have to self-consciously erect a structure to replace the body, not just to extend it. In his Catholic thinking, the body becomes the site not of lived experience, but of sin, and the proper way to behave becomes to live according to the norms of nature:

The homosexual was sinful because he had no kosher place to stick it. In attempting to drape the architecture of sodomy with art, homosexuals have lived for thousands of years against the expectations of nature. Barren as Shakers and, interestingly, as concerned with the small effect, homosexuals have made a covenant against nature. Homosexual survival lay in artifice, in plumage, in lampshades, sonnets, musical comedy, couture, syntax, religious ceremony, opera, lacquer, irony.[4]

Out of this queer taste came a new form of perverse space:

Taste, which is, after all, the insecurity of the middle class, became the homosexual's licentiate to challenge the rules of nature. . . . The impulse is not to create but to re-create, to sham, to convert, to sauce, to rouge, to fragrance, to prettify. No effect is too small or too ephemeral to be snatched away from nature, to be ushered toward the perfection of artificiality. . . . In San Francisco in the 1980s, the highest form of art became interior decoration. The glory hole was thus converted to an eighteenth-century foyer.[5]

This fantastical space, built out of the very insecurity of the middle class and erected with all the mirroring pose of the queer man, became so complete as to establish not just a second nature, which is already all of the man-made environment, but a third nature, a kind of fiction of the man-made. It brought out the long tradition of the rococo elaboration of artifice into a mirroring of artifice, a movement that had developed from dandyism and collecting, through aestheticism and decadence, through Arts and Crafts revelations and interior dream worlds, into the elaborate fictions of the disco and the bathhouse.

The problem with this construction was that it had no content in any real experience. Queer space was a heavily guarded and decorated void. It was this emptiness that defeated queer culture, and AIDS was no more than a reminder of this emptiness: "AIDS, it has been discovered, is a plague of absence. Absence opened in the blood. Absence condensed into the fluid of passing emotion. Absence shot through opalescent tugs of semen to deflower the city."[6]

This is a cruel analysis, and comes close to the argument of the semifascist right that queers deserved to die because they broke the laws of both man and nature. Rodriguez removes the argument from a notion of blame and merely points out that AIDS is an extreme case of the way in which our culture threatens continually to fall prey to the very body it tries to repress. As travel, medical technology, and more and more complicated social structures open up new spaces, they also make us more vulnerable. They reveal the void of human existence.

2

The queerest space of all is the void,
and AIDS has made us live that emptiness, that absence, that loss. More than any war or epidemic, more than any crime or social injustice, AIDS has revealed the open space at the heart of American society. It is not a queer space any of us would want to inhabit, but many have been forced to make it their own.

AIDS did not kill all queers, nor did it end the continuing effort to build queer spaces. It did not even end the contributions queer spaces have made to the transformation of the urban environment. Out of both the struggle against AIDS and the memories that culture of loss let loose in our world have come new queer spaces. They are empty, unreal places, and as such might even be models for a society whose places themselves are becoming more and more unreal: queer space might be the space of electronic networks, a space to be surfed and cruised and connected to not through real experience, but through the mask of technology.

Figure 5.1
Lola Flash,
*AIDS Quilt–
The First Year,
1991*

The most famous space of AIDS is that acres of memory that unfolded, first on the lawn of the Capitol and then on squares all around the world, in the form of the Quilt. This collage of memories became a spatial equivalent of what was lost. It placed itself in the tradition of women creating a community within and through the constraints placed on them by men, by weaving the bits and scraps of everyday life into a cloak of comfort. Making the quilt, not its use, was in many cases more important. Instead of the proud monuments of those who had fought wars, the quilt became as ephemeral, portable, and insinuating as queer spaces themselves. It was a decorative monument that condensed the lives of all of those who died within the wars urban culture unleashed on itself.

Several architects have tried to make the experience of queer space into a self-conscious construction. Mark Robbins had moved from the design of little altarpieces to the male nude, surrounded by mementos and *memento mori*, to the fabrication of analogs to the tearooms and sex clubs that hide within the proper architectural scene. Robbins undresses buildings into their skeletons and most naked elements, including pipes, grates, and concrete blocks. He arranges these rough, usually hidden materials into cubicles that mimic the rational orders of buildings, and then penetrates them with peep fissures, glory holes, and moments where the solid wall suddenly disappears at crotch height to open the user up to view and use. This is a queer space that defies absence with its naked presence.

Figure 5.2b
Mark Robbins,
New York:
Angles of
Incidence,
1991

Durham Crout, on the other hand, has proposed building similar structures of obscenity, but here they are literally marked with the names of all those who might have used them, but now are dead. It is a monument to AIDS that reconstructs the very obscenity in which the disease appeared, and glorifies it as a place that still is worth constructing. This kind of proud erection that is shot through with both a sense of loss and a pornographic pleasure in naked materials is becoming widespread among queer architects trying to make sense out of their world in the age of AIDS. It marks a coming out of the closet of them as designers and queers, a dual identity that reinforces itself in the installation of a critical architecture.

The art of AIDS is by now substantial. Much of it is militant, designed only to shock or persuade. This very shock has had an effect on the city. It has forced straight inhabitants to confront a gritty reality that is not the domain of some other group, but is the one we have all made together. When ACT UP began asserting the presence of queers in the city, using the name that until then had been mainly a term of derision as an emblem of pride, they did more than argue in a forceful way for the necessity of more funding for AIDS research. They made queerness visible. This was not a visibility that made queerness respectable or gave it its proper place, but rather one that laid bare the pervasiveness of queer life. It was as if a double trace had suddenly come to light in many American cities: the shadow city of queerness that exploited places of business, empty lots, and roads for sexual acts, and the network of the disease that laid itself over these acts.

Figure 5.3
Durham Crout,
Wasting
Architecture,
1993

Artists such as David Wojnarowicz made their art out of this tracing. In a series of photocollages produced at the end of his life, Wojnarowicz superimposed queer men engaged in having sex on negative images of the city. He also overlaid scenes of forests around these acts, as if the city were a jungle teeming with both sensual delights and danger. Cartoon figures floated around urban moonscapes, and ancient emblems of queer suffering such as Saint Sebastian took their place against a backdrop of dollar bills. Icons of work, begging, and supernatural power confronted the viewer with a colorful distraction from pornographic scenes in the same paintings. Giant ants cruised up naked torsos and around eyeballs, queering the body. Throughout these stark images, Wojnarowicz's own words spelled out his search for sex and salvation in a city that for him had an operatic sensibility. Finally, his work became decorative, disappearing into text and colors. All that remains is figures wearing masks, as if both art and identity are making do with their provisional nature. Art here did not elaborate loss: loss becomes an art that elaborates itself in the city.

In a sense Wojnarowicz's work continued itself beyond the frame and his life in the graffiti spread through the city, marking the shadows of lost friends on walls and pavement, reminding us that "silence = death" and bringing the obscenity of absence to life in everyday streets. AIDS might have been as invisible as queers have often been, but its appearance among this outcast group left marks that remained as apparent as the lesions on a victim's face. This was not a plague one could exile into hospitals or internment camps, despite the suggestion of the far right. This was disease that brought the city back to itself. The marks of AIDS, in art and in the streets, appeared after the last great operatic explosion of middle-class lust that transformed American cities into gleaming towers hovering over abandoned streets, and made us understand the gap between the dreams of continual (self-)development and the reality of daily suffering.

Figure 5.4a
David Wojnarowicz,
Untitled,
from *Sex Series,*
1988–1989

"All my life," said Wojnarowicz, "I've made things that are like fragmented mirrors of what I perceive the world to be."[7] At first, that vision was liberating:

> *I lean down and find the neckline of his sweater and draw it back and away from the nape of his neck which I gently probe with my tongue. In loving him, I saw a cigarette between the fingers of a hand, smoke blowing backwards into the room, and sputtering planes diving low through the clouds. In loving him, I saw men encouraging each other to lay down their arms. In loving him, I saw small-town laborers creating excavations that other men spend their lives trying to fill. In loving him, I saw moving films of stone buildings; I saw a hand in prison dragging snow in from the sill. In loving him, I saw great houses being erected that would soon slide into the waiting and stirring seas. I saw him freeing me from the silences of interior life.[8]*

But now "death comes in small doses":

Some days this room becomes an architecture of fear when the sun goes down. The night comes down between the buildings and presses itself around the moldings of the windowframes, spreading itself across and through the glass. It becomes thick and textural. What I feel is the momentary shock of realizing that most of the wood, metal and plastic fixtures, the sinks, lampshades, the shower stall, and even the drinking cups will all outlive me if my body follows the progression that this tiny, invisible-to-the-eye virus has initiated. Time reveals itself to be a childlike notion of false structure. The social landscape I have grown to be comforted by is being exploded and is disappearing.[9]

This dissolution is also a homecoming: "Where once I felt acutely alien, now it's more like an immersion in a body of warm water and the water that surrounds me is air, is breathing, is life itself. I'm acutely aware of myself aware and listening."[10]

Figure 5.4b
David Wojnarowicz,
Bad Moon Rising,
1989

3

The other side of this harsh medicine was the bittersweet landscapes of memory that appeared as queers turned back inward. Queer literature, which had been a growing field since the publication of Gore Vidal's *The City and the Pillar* in 1948, exploded in the late 1980s. Writers such as Edmund White and Paul Monette used their own life history to evoke a world that was almost mythic in its achievements. These were stories of quest, like much great literature, but the goal was not the obtainment of a symbol of salvation, love, or riches. Rather, it was a meandering drift through life in search for the self, as Rechy had already pointed out. The queer quest was one whose space was not linear, but labyrinthine. It did not lead to the fulfillment of a dream and the achievement of a new life, but rather mirrored life in the artifice of a newly found gay identity.

Much of this literature was repetitive in its structure. It recounted the trials and tribulations of adolescence, the first great love, the hidden moments of sex, and a sense of fulfillment usually not through an achievement of a state of bliss or married stability, but exactly through loss. Almost all of the books end with deaths, drownings, or abandonments that turn the narrator back toward himself drifting through the city. Again as Rechy had pointed out, for these queer men, the city was enough. It was, in the words of one commentator, a "state of desire" that continued through time and place even as faces changed. This is the key to the anonymity of much queer culture: since it is always seeking the self in sameness, through posing one's self in self-created stage sets, it never finds anything but itself continually searching. Queer space becomes an awareness of the emptiness within the city that does not defeat but animates one's self to always go searching.

Matthew Stadler describes that state in a city that is both specific in time and place and mythic, where ancient emblems and modern conveniences mix in a version of Seattle. Police and parents haunt the narrator as he tries to construct a self, in one book literally by building masks, and in another by tracing the operatic constructions of the seventeenth century. He never finds fulfillment, only disappearance and loss, as his loves always die, disappear, or are kept away from him by the law.[11]

At its best, this absence becomes metaphysical, as it does for the English writer Alan Hollinghurst in bringing back the memories of his adolescence:

> *My favorite time was soon after sunset, when I liked to catch the first sight of the evening star, suddenly bright, high in the west above the darkening outlines of the copses. It was a solitary ritual, wound up incoherently with bits of poetry said over and over like spells: sunset and evening star, the star that bids the shepherd fold, her fond yellow hornlight wound to the west. . . . It intensified and calmed my yearnings at the same time, like a song. In one poem I'd seen that first star referred to as the folding star, and the words haunted me with their suggestion of something ancient but evanescent; I look up to it in a mood of desolate solitude burning into cold calm. I lingered, testing out the ache of it: I had to be back before it was truly dark, but in high summer that could be very late. I became a connoisseur of the last lonely gradings of blue into black.*[12]

This embrace of yearning floats through queer literature, intensified by a sense of loss and the impossibility of integration with everyday life. It gives an opening toward mythic landscapes that remain closed to those searching for a rational space of belonging within the metropolis. It was reiterated by Derek Jarman not long before his death:

> *The image is a prison of the soul, your heredity, your education, your vices and aspirations, your qualities, your psychological world. I have walked behind the sky. For what are you seeking? The fathomless blue of Bliss. To be an astronaut of the void, leave the comfortable house that imprisons you with reassurance. Remember, to be going and to have are not eternal—fight the fear that engenders the beginning, the middle and the end. For Blue there are no boundaries or solutions.*[13]

4

Beyond such romantic constructions, queer space has very little left to offer to either queers or straights in a concrete manner.

Queer space is, in fact, in danger of disappearing.

AIDS destroyed the queer community as a coherent structure, and queers disappeared into their homes, the suburbs, and anonymity. Even condoms and other forms of safe sex came between bodies, making the sexual act itself less intense. Now queers often want to be normal. They adopt children, dress like their neighbors, and even disavow the presence of a communal culture. When they gather in suburban bars or support groups, those places are no different from the few spaces "affinity groups" have carved out within the formless sprawl of our cities. They are bare meeting rooms, places of confession, or places of therapy. Only occasionally do queers still come together to celebrate their pride, but even these festivals and parades have lost their intensity, their obnoxious difference, their queerness. Even drag is now a consumer phenomenon, as is the desire for underage boys that to queer authors like Dennis Cooper laid bare the rootlessness and moral boundlessness of suburbia in an extremely violent and spatial manner. Now it is just a Calvin Klein ad.

The only remaining place of resistance appears to be the electronic bulletin boards, chat groups, and pornography sites on the World Wide Web. There queers gather in anonymity, wearing electronic masks and creating artificial lives. They revel in the freedom of the Web more than any other group, and weave connections that sometimes translate into meetings for sex or friendship. To them, cruising the Web becomes a safe-sex version of cruising the city. Like the cyberpunks in William Gibson's books, they live their lives in a plane that extends along neural nets that penetrate the shell of the body without much resistance. Queer cyberpunks are moving beyond the body, beyond community, and beyond sex to the orgasm of electronic impulses constructing fantastic universes.

5

There is not much stability in such places, nor is there a sense of being alive in the real world. What is even more important, straight society is no more than a nanosecond behind queers in their colonization of this last queer space. Already the obscenity of the Web is under scrutiny or, alternately, development by commercial spaces. It remains therefore to be seen whether this can become a queer space that is productive.

For queer space has been productive.

It has shown all of us how to create identities that depend on real experiences and connections with other humans to create a community that is not dependent on institutions or clichés, but that is an ephemeral, woven network of belonging that allows us to cruise through the continually changing landscape of the modern metropolis. Queer space is not one place: it is an act of appropriating the modern world for the continual act of self-construction. It is obscene and artificial by its very nature. It creates its own beauty. It allows us to be alive in a world of technology. There we can continually search within ourselves as we mirror ourselves in the world for that self that has a body, a desire, a life. Queer space queers reality to produce a space to live.

I am reminded of Michel Foucault's proposal that what we need in our society is "heterotopias":

> *There also exist, and this is probably true for all cultures and all civilizations, real and effective spaces which are outlined in the very institution of society, but which constitute a sort of counter-arrangement of effectively realized utopia, in which all the real arrangements, all the other real arrangements that can be found within society, are at one and the same time represented, challenged and overturned: a sort of place that lies outside all places and yet is actually localizable.[14]*

An example of such a space
would be the mirror:

. . . it is a place without a place. In it, I see myself where I am not, in an unreal space that opens up potentially beyond its surface; there I am down there where I am not, a sort of shadow that makes my appearance visible to myself, allowing me to look at myself where I do not exist. . . . Hence the mirror functions as a heterotopia, since it makes the place that I occupy, whenever I look myself in the glass, both absolutely real— it is in fact linked to all the surrounding space—and absolutely unreal, for in order to be perceived it has of necessity to pass that virtual point that is situated down there.[15]

Heterotopias function in our society as mirrors to our culture. They become condensed modes of mirroring where we pass beyond the bounds of time and place without leaving those spaces. Men's and women's houses were once such heterotopias, says Foucault, and the palaces of culture now function to make us see ourselves. They are mirror spaces that open up in everyday experience. Heterotopias are ultimately places of construction, both of the self and of society. His final models are colonies and brothels: places of appropriation and artificial creation, places of sinking into a communal embrace of ephemeral realization. We need such heterotopias, such queer spaces:

Brothels and colonies, here are two extreme types of heterotopia. Think of the ship: it is a floating part of space, a placeless place, that lives by itself, closed in on itself and at the same time poised in the infinite ocean, and yet, from port to port, tack by tack, from brothel to brothel, it goes as far as the colonies, looking for the most precious things hidden in their gardens. . . . The ship is the heterotopia par excellence. In civilizations where it is lacking, dreams dry up, adventure is replaced by espionage and privateers by police.[16]

Cruising through the city or cyberspace, the queer privateers move from their operatic colonies to the dirty delights of sex clubs, opening up the tightly packed, floating communal oval of a ship, a queer ark always looking for a port. I hope it remains always afloat.

Notes

Introduction *Some Queer Constructs*

1 Prince, "1999," ASCAP, 1982.

2 I especially want to try to avoid psychoanalytic readings of history, such as those that would identify and retroactively out figures ranging from Alexander the Great to Abraham Lincoln. This seems to be the major thrust of much current popular writing on the history of homosexuality.

3 Aaron Betsky, *Building Sex: Men, Women, Architecture, and the Construction of Sexuality* (New York: William Morrow, 1995).

4 Virginia Frankel, *What Your House Tells About You* (New York: Trident Press, 1972).

5 The term "homosexual" entered the English lexicon only in the late nineteenth century, and became the "polite" word for those who engaged in same-sex acts or had same-sex desires (two terms the current political regime is trying to further separate). "Gay" is one of a series of phrases appropriated by such men and women in the nineteenth century, while "queer" became the favorite term of the post-AIDS generation. I have chosen the last phrase. My only justification is that it echoes the notion that the spaces I am discussing here are somehow odd, unusual, or haunting.

I admit, however, that there is a method to this choice: it implies a movement from unnamed safe sex desires through the stigma of homosexuality and the self-conscious celebration of gayness to the aggressive claims of Queer Nation, which "locates the public space in which the individual Cartesian subject must be out, transforming that space in order to survive. Queer Nation's design maps a psychic and bodily territory—lavender territory—that cannot be colonized and expands it to include, potentially, the entire nation." Lauren Berlant and Elizabeth Freeman, "Queer Nationality," *Boundary 2*, Vol. 19, No. 1 (Spring 1992), pp.149–80, 161. See also Alessandra Stanley, "Militants Back 'Queer,' Showing 'Gay' the Way of 'Negro,' *New York Times*, April 6, 1991, pp. 23–24.

6 The core of this discussion is not so much to be found in the epochal *Capital* as in the earlier and more philosophical *Economic and Philosophical Manuscripts of 1844*, ed. Dirk J. Struiker, trans. Martin Milligan (New York: International Publishers, 1964), esp. pp. 106–69.

7 Thus the art historian T. J. Clark has argued that the central effort of bourgeois art was to convert a city of production into a city of spectacle for the middle classes, a place of controlled experience governed by the artifice of both the state (which laid out the streets) and the artist, who pictured their life as a unity. T. J. Clark, *The Painting of Modern Life: Paris in the Art of Manet and His Followers* (New York: Alfred A. Knopf, 1985).

8 Cf. Eve Kosofsky Sedgwick, *Epistemology of the Closet* (Berkeley: University of California Press, 1990).

9 Walter Benjamin remains the most trenchant observer of this world, both in his "Passagen" fragments and especially in "Paris, Capital of the Nineteenth Century," in *Reflections: Essays, Aphorisms, Autobiographical Writings*, trans. Edmund Jephcott (New York: Schocken Books, 1978), pp. 146–62.

Chapter 1 *Closet Cases and Mirror Worlds*

1 Richard Rodriguez, *Days of Obligation: An Argument with My Mexican Father* (New York: Penguin Books, 1992), p. 30.

2 Though Eve Kosofsky Sedgwick's *Epistemology of the Closet* (Berkeley: University of California Press, 1990) dances around what exactly the closet is or contains (esp. pp. 71ff), she never really defines her terms in this case. The philosopher Gaston Bachelard (*The Poetics of Space*, trans. Maria Jolas [Boston: Beacon Press, 1994] also discusses the closet, but he sees it (pp. 78–79) as the very emblem and heart of domestic order.

3 Nor, according to Jacques Lacan, could you ever imagine constituting yourself as anything but an infantile creature in the "mirror-stage." To construct a self through "aggressivity" that challenges the ego in an other remains the principal task of the alienated individual. Lacan proposes that only "suicide" allows any escape from this schema; he dismisses homosexuality as infantile. See Jacques Lacan, "The Mirror Stage as Formative of the Function of the I as Revealed in Psychoanalytic Experience," pp. 1–7, and "Aggressivity in Psychoanalysis," pp. 8–27, in *Écrits: A Selection*, trans. Alan Sheridan (New York: W. W. Norton, 1977).

4 For a good account of the meaning of sadomasochism that condenses both primary and secondary sources, see James Miller, *The Passion of Michel Foucault* (New York: Anchor Books, 1993), pp. 260–84.

5 Cf. Michel Foucault, "Other Spaces: The Principles of Heterotopia," *Lotus* 48/49 (1986), pp. 10–24.

6 The importance of gesture in the making of space is discussed most fully by Henri Lefebvre in his *The Production of Space*, trans. Donald Nicholson-Smith (Oxford: Blackwell, 1991 [1974]), pp. 169ff.

7 This will be discussed more fully in Chapter 5 below. See Edward William Delph, *The Silent Community: Public Homosexual Encounters* (Beverly Hills, Calif.: Sage Publications, 1978), esp. p. 23.

8 Gestural buildings are a special favorite of the architect and theoretician Robert Venturi (see Chapter 4), who wrote about them in his *Complexity and Contradiction in Architecture* (New York: Museum of Modern Art, 1966).

9 Jim Fourratt, in Arthur Bell, Jim Fouratt, Kate Millet, Vito Russo, Jeff Weinstein, Edmund White, and Bertha Harris, "Extended Sensibilities: The Impact of Homosexual Sensibilities on Contemporary Culture," in Russell Ferguson, William Olander, Marcia Tucker, and Karen Fiss, eds., *Discourses: Conversations in Postmodern Art and Culture* (New York: New Museum of Contemporary Art, 1990), pp. 130–53, p. 134.

10 Anthony Vidler, "The Scenes of the Street: Transformations in Ideal and Reality, 1750–1871," in Stanford Anderson, ed., *On Streets* (Cambridge, Mass.: MIT Press, 1986 [1978]), pp. 29–32.

11 Margaret Mead, *Male and Female: A Study of the Sexes in a Changing World* (New York: Morrow Quill Paperbacks, 1977 [1949]), pp. 93–94. Mead points out that this particular society is one with no discernible homosexual practices.

12 Cf. Gerald W. Creed, "Sexual Subordination: Institutionalized Homosexuality and Social Control in Melanesia," in Jonathan Goldberg, ed., *Reclaiming Sodom* (New York: Routledge, 1994), pp. 66–94; Daphne Spain, *Gendered Spaces* (Chapel Hill, N.C.: University of North Carolina Press, 1992), pp. 67–79.

Chapter 1 *Closet Cases and Mirror Worlds*

13 For a good example of this Papua New Guinea, see Gilbert H. Herdt, *Guardians of the Flutes: Idioms of Masculinity* (New York: McGraw-Hill, 1981), pp. 32ff.

14 Cf. David F. Greenberg, *The Construction of Homosexuality* (Chicago: University of Chicago Press, 1988), pp. 38ff.

15 Elizabeth Weatherford describes such places as allowing men and women to define their own culture, thus establishing separate realms that yet remain open to each other. Elizabeth Weatherford, "Women's Traditional Architecture," in *Heresies* 2 (1977), pp. 35–39.

16 These are the areas that have been most intensively studied by the sources cited by Creed, Spain, and Greenberg. Unfortunately, the descriptions of actual spaces remains exceedingly sparse. It appears that the evidence for most "compulsory homosexuality" (as Creed terms it) is anecdotal and tied to observation or to acts, not places or things. This marks the overall problem for the definition of queer space, namely that it must be defined by inference from fleeting acts, rather than from the establishment of fixed and observable phenomena.

17 Ernest Guidoni, *Primitive Architecture*, trans. Robert Erich Wolf (New York: Rizzoli/Electa, 1987 [1975], p. 48.

18 My discussion here is derived from Vincent Scully's *The Earth, the Temple, and the Gods: Greek Sacred Architecture* (New York: Praeger, 1969), though this emphasis on order is, of course, subjective and colored by the importance of Greek architecture as a model for later formal developments.

19 The Greek *gymnos* means naked.

20 Richard Sennett, *Flesh and Stone: The Body and the City in Western Civilization* (New York: W. W. Norton, 1994), pp. 44ff.

21 Ibid., p. 50.

22 Ibid., p. 77.

23 Cf. Eva C. Keuls, *The Reign of the Phallus: Sexual Politics in Ancient Athens* (New York: Harper & Row, 1985).

24 It is this very "fictional" quality that also marked a woman's space, as she could reinvent herself there. See Marilyn B. Arthur, "The Dream of a World Without Women: Poetics and the Circles of Order in the *Theogony* Prooemium," *Arethusa*, Vol. 16, Nos. 1, 2 (1983), pp. 97–116; Sennett, p. 77.

25 Cf. Aaron Betsky, *Building Sex: Men, Women, Architecture, and the Construction of Sexuality* (New York: William Morrow, 1995), pp. 64–83.

26 "From their inception in Classical Greece the public baths were censured for their appeal to sensual pleasure, and they were accorded a place at the other end of the moral scale from the gymnasium. Baths were associated with an effete and wasteful lifestyle, which was said to have ensnared the well-born youth of Aristophanes's Athens." Fikret Yegül, *Baths and Bathing in Classical Antiquity* (New York: Architectural History Foundation, 1992), p. 41. There was also a certain eroticism about the very public aspect of the bath: "In analyzing the emotional fantasies of [Michel Neiri's] childhood, he was to attribute the voluptuous, erotic excitement he derived from it to the cruelty and the 'bathroom aspect of its architecture, the glacial marble with its suggestion of sweating rooms, skin beaded with tiny drops, spirals of steam, naked bodies.' Perhaps the nearest equivalents these days to the steamy atmosphere of the ancient baths, now that the New York bath-houses have gone, are those basements of certain Hamburg hotels, where on velvet sofas by the sides of green marble pools naked sirens offer up their charms among potted palms and *papier mâché* pillars." Charles Sprawson, *Haunts of the Black Masseur: The Swimmer as Hero* (New York: Penguin Books, 1994), p. 48.

27 Ibid., p. 183.

28 Ibid., p. 5.

29 Ibid., p. 2.

30 John Boswell, *Christianity, Social Tolerance and Homosexuality: Gay People in Western Europe from the Beginning of the Christian Era to the Fourteenth Century* (Chicago: University of Chicago Press, 1980), p. 38.

31 For a good synopsis of the current (highly speculative) state of research on homosexuality during this period, see Paul Halsall, "The Experience of Homosexuality in the Middle Ages," manuscript posted on the World Wide Web. The difficulties are made even larger by the lack of understanding about the meaning of key phrases, so that we are left interpreting the implications of acts and declarations of love without being able to clearly assign same-sex activity.

32 Boswell, p. 35. Boswell has continued his discussion in his more recent *Same Sex Unions in Pre-Modern Europe* (New York: Random House, 1994).

33 For a fuller discussion of female mystics and their lesbian imagery, see Catherine Walker Bynum, *Fragmentation and Redemption: Essays on Gender and the Human Body in Medieval Religion* (New York: Zone Books, 1991).

34 Greenberg, pp. 282–86.

35 Sennett, p. 228.

36 It is interesting to note the relationship between queers, Jews, and capitalism: all three were seen as embodying a secret network that spread through the fabric of society. See Chapter 4.

37 Eve Kosofsky Sedgwick, *op.cit.*, discusses the breakdown of the distinction between public and private space in her treatment of Melville's *Billy Budd*, pp. 110–11.

38 This was the position made most famous by Jean Genet in such stories as *The Miracle of the Rose*, in the *Selected Writings of Jean Genet*, trans. Bernard Frechtman (Hopewell, N.J.: Ecco Press, 1993 [1949]), pp. 50–108, in which he claims that "it is the rigors of prison that drive us toward each other in bursts of love without which we could not live" (p. 51) and speaks of the "splendid debauchery" that takes place in these grim places (p. 89).

39 Cf. Manfredo Tafuri, " 'The Wicked Architect': G. B. Piranesi, Heterotopia, and the Voyage," in *The Sphere and the Labyrinth: Avant Gardes and Architectures from Piranesi to the 1970s*, trans. Pellegrino D'Acierno and Robert Connolly (Cambridge, Mass.: MIT Press, 1990 [1980]), pp. 25–54.

40 This order resembled the prison in that it was designed to be able to police the inhabitants and prevent their sexual experimentation—giving the whole a sexually charged atmosphere. The writer Alisdare Hickson has divided these mechanisms of control into demarcation, denunciation, diversion, defeminization, debarment (of "feminized" races), detection, and deterrence, and has shown how these very actions created highly charged atmospheres where the concentration on the body (in pools and gymnasia) and its abnegation (in chapels) heightened the focus on and desire for flesh in English boarding schools. Alisdare Hickson, *The Poisoned Bowl: Sex, Repression and the Public School System* (London: Constable and Company, 1995). See also Michel Foucault, *The History of Sexuality: An Introduction*, trans. Robert Hurley (New York: Vintage Books, 1978), Vol. 1, pp. 27–29.

Chapter 1 *Closet Cases and Mirror Worlds*

41 The various informants cited by Hickson (*op. cit.*) point out that "everyone knows that these schools, such as the Rugby I attended, are rife with homosexual activity, which has not precluded the vast majority of people, on leaving these schools, from having heterosexual affairs, and even marrying eventually" (p. 175). The question remains how important such queer relations were in the bonding process that made these schools so important in the establishment of the centralized moral and financial control systems of the British Empire. How important, in other words, is sexual attraction in the old boys' network? What, moreover, is the importance of the physical spaces of its schools—shaped, as noted above, to a large degree by the policing of sexual activity—as models for institutional and private memories that spread throughout the empire?

42 Cf. Bonnie S. Anderson and Judith P. Zinsser, *A History of Their Own: Women in Europe from Prehistory to the Present* (New York: Perennial Books, 1988), Vol. 2, pp. 114ff.

43 John Cleland, *Memoirs of a Woman of Pleasure* (New York: Oxford University Press, 1985 [1749]). The one passage describing sodomy was excised from the text for more than a century.

44 Marquis de Sade, *The 120 Days of Sodom and Other Writing*, trans. Austryn Wainhouse and Richard Seaver (New York: Grove Weidenfeld, 1966).

45 This has become a trope of neo-Lacanian philosophy. For a discussion of the centrality of "sodomitical acts" in de Sade, see Pierre Klossowski, "The Philosopher-Villain," in Goldberg, pp. 221–46.

46 De Sade, pp. 237–38.

Chapter 2 *Aesthetic Escapades and Escapes*

1 William Beckford, *Vathek* (New York: Oxford University Press, 1983 [1786]), p. 2.

2 Theo van der Meer, "Sodomy and the Pursuit of a Third Sex in the Early Modern Period," in Gilbert Herdt, ed., *Third Sex, Third Gender: Beyond Sexual Dimorphism in Culture and History* (New York: Zone Books, 1994), pp. 137–212; see also Simon Schama, *The Embarrassment of Riches: An Interpretation of Dutch Culture in the Golden Age* (Berkeley: University of California Press, 1988), pp. 601–66.

3 Svetlana Alpers, *The Art of Describing: Dutch Art in the Seventeenth Century* (Chicago: University of Chicago Press, 1983).

4 Svetlana Alpers, "Seeing as Knowing: A Dutch Connection," in *Humanities in Society* I (1978), pp. 147–173.

5 Van der Meer, pp. 211–12.

6 Ibid., p. 151.

7 Such cruising grounds again traced the emerging spaces of the middle class, incuding the parks, the theater, and the coffee houses. For a good summary of fairly current scholarship, see David F. Greenberg, *The Construction of Homosexuality* (Chicago: University of Chicago Press, 1988), pp. 301–46.

8 "Sexual relations between two males were similarly illegal, immoral and yet honorable when conducted in ways that displayed adult male power. In most of Europe and certainly in England, this was achieved when adult males sexually penetrated adolescent boys, who existed in a transitional state between man and woman. All men were supposed to be capable of such acts with boys. . . . These sexual relations between men and boys did not—and this is the essential point—carry with them the stigma of effeminacy or of inappropriate behavior, as they began to do after 1700 and have continued to ever since in modern Western societies." Randolph Trumbach, "Erotic Fantasy and Male Libertinism in Enlightenment England," in Lynn Hunt, ed., *The Invention of Pornography: Obscenity and the Origins of Modernity, 1500–1800* (New York: Zone Books, 1993), pp. 253–82, pp. 254–55. See also Jonathan Goldberg, ed., *Queering the Renaissance* (Durham, N.C.: Duke University Press, 1994), esp. Jonathan Goldberg, "Introduction," pp. 1–14, and Alan Bray, "Homosexuality and the Signs of Male Friendship in Elizabethan England," pp. 40–61.

9 E. M. Forster, *Maurice* (New York: W. W. Norton, 1992 [1914]), pp. 92–93, 244.

10 For a discussion of the variety of roles available to queers in the nineteenth century, see Alan Sinfield, *The Wilde Century: Effeminacy, Oscar Wilde and the Queer Movement* (London: Cassell, 1994), esp. pp. 30ff.

11 Cf. Michel Foucault, *The History of Sexuality: An Introduction*, trans. Robert Hurley (New York: Vintage Books, 1978), Vol. 1, pp. 15ff; Elizabeth Wilson, *The Sphinx in the City: Urban Life, the Control of Disorder, and Women.* (Berkeley, Calif.: University of California Press, 1992).

12 Mario Praz, *An Illustrated History of Interior Decoration from Pompeii to Art Nouveau* (London: Thames & Hudson, 1981 [1964]), pp. 24–25.

13 Sinfield, p. 53.

14 Ibid., p. 64.

15 William Beckford, *Vathek* (New York: Oxford University Press, 1983 [1786]).

16 This fantastic novel obviously takes its place in the rising fad of Orientalism which, as Edward Said has so ably pointed out, allowed middle-class men in the nineteenth century to construct an image of a place that contained all the qualities of sensuality and submission they sought to find at home, while keeping alive the notion of a mysterious "other" that validated one's rationalizing labors. Edward Said, in his book *Orientalism* (New York: Vintage Books, 1979), connects Beckford's tastes, significantly, with "Piranesi's prisons. . . Tiepolo's luxurious ambiences. . . the exotic sublimity of late-nineteenth-century painting" (p. 118). For a good discussion of *Vathek*, see Kenneth W. Graham, ed., *Vathek and The Escape from Time. Bicentenary Revaluations* (New York: AMS Press, 1990).

17 For a full description of these structures, see James Lees-Milne, *William Beckford* (London: Compton Russell, 1976).

18 Ibid., p. 60.

19 Ibid., p. 62.

20 In 1822, Beckford sold Fonthill and its contents to John Farquhar for the then immense sum of £330,000. This and the collections he later amassed at Bath became the foundation of several important private and public holdings in antiques and rare books.

21 Letter by William Beckford, quoted in Roger Lonsdale, "Introduction," in *Vathek*, pp. xv–xxxi, pp. xi–xii.

22 There are few recent biographies of Ludwig II. The best in the English language remains Katerina van der Burg's *Ludwig II of Bavaria: The Man and the Mystery* (Windsor, UK: Windsor Publications, 1989).

23 For a good description of Ludwig's architectural projects, see Roy Strong and Lisa Taylor, eds., *Designs for the Dream King: The Castles and Palaces of Ludwig II of Bavaria* (London: Debrett's Peerage Ltd., 1978), and especially the essay by Simon Jervis, "Ludwig II of Bavaria: His Architecture, Design and Decoration in Context," pp. 9–21.

24 Jervis, p. 15.

25 Ibid., p. 20.

26 T. J. Jackson Lears, "Infinite Riches in a Little Room: The Interior Scenes of Modernist Culture," *Modulus* 18 (1987), pp. 3–27, p. 9.

27 I am here reminded of the use such French writers as Jacques Lacan and Luce Irigary have made of the notion of *jouissance,* which in the original has overtones of sexual indulgence (*jouir* is slang for "to come").

28 Joris-Karl Huysmans, *Against Nature*, trans. Robert Baldick (New York: Penguin Books, 1959 [1884]), p. 25.

29 Ibid., p. 36.

30 Ibid., p. 22.

31 Ibid., pp. 70ff.

32 Ibid., p. 75.

33 Ibid., p. 111.

34 Edouard Roditi, *Oscar Wilde* (New York: New Directions, 1986), pp. 140ff; Richard Ellman, *Oscar Wilde* (New York: Alfred A. Knopf, 1988).

35 Moe Meyer, "Under the Sign of Wilde: An Archaeology of Posing," in Moe Meyer, *The Politics and Poetics of Camp* (London: Routledge, 1994), pp. 75–109, p. 77.

36 Ibid., p. 82.

37 For a fuller description of Wildean aesthetics, see Stephen Calloway, " 'The Dandyism of the Senses': Aesthetic Ideals and Decadent Attitudes in the 1890s," in Michael Spense, ed., *The Studio: High Art and Low Life: "The Studio" and the Fin-de-Siècle* (London: Victoria and Albert Museum, 1993), pp. 55–63.

38 Cf. Vyvyan Holland, *Son of Oscar Wilde* (New York: E. P. Dutton, 1954), p. 17.

39 Ibid.

40 Richard Butler Gleanzer, ed., *Decorative Art in America: A Lecture by Oscar Wilde, Together with Letters, Reviews and Interviews* (New York: Brentano's, 1906).

41 Susan Sontag, "Notes on Camp," in *A Susan Sontag Reader* (New York: Farrar, Straus & Giroux, 1982 [1964]), pp. 105–19, p. 116. This short essay has become central in defining what we think of as queer style, as it links notions of aestheticism, artifice, and homosexuality.

42 Gleanzer, p. 4.

43 Ibid., p. 5.

44 Sontag, pp. 108–10.

45 For the most cogent statement of these ideas, see John Ruskin, "The Two Paths in Art; Being Lectures on Art, and Its Application to Decoration and Manufacture, Delivered in 1858–9," in *The Works of John Ruskin*, Vol. 12 (New York: John Wiley & Sons, 1879).

46 Alan Crawford, *C. R. Ashbee: Architect, Designer and Romantic Socialist* (New Haven, Conn.: Yale University Press, 1985), p. 41.

47 Ibid., p. 161.

48 Ibid., p. 212.

49 Ibid., pp. 22ff.

50 For a nearly contemporary model for such a place, see Esther Newton, *Cherry Grove, Fire Island: Sixty Years in America's First Gay and Lesbian Town* (New York: Beacon Books, 1993).

51 Gelett Burgess, *The Romance of the Commonplace* (San Francisco: P. Elder & M. Shepard, 1902), pp. 128–32), quoted in Douglass Shand-Tucci, *Boston Bohemia 1881–1900*, Vol. 1 of *Ralph Adams Cram: Life and Architecture* (Amherst, Mass.: University of Massachusetts Press, 1995).

52 For a highly refined version of this process, one might look at the work of the very fashionable Atlanta architect Philip Shutze, who was an inveterate collector and appropriator of classic styles. Shutze preferred baroque and flowing forms and grand furniture, but tamed his own interests in favor of the less adventurous tastes of his clients, while holding on to an expressive refinement that still sets his work apart. See Elizabeth Meredith Dowling, *American Classicist: The Architecture of Philip Trammell Shutze* (New York: Rizzoli Publications, 1989).

53 T. J. Jackson Lears, *No Place of Grace: Antimodernism and the Transformation of American Culture, 1880–1920* (New York: Pantheon, 1981), pp. 59–96, 203–7.

54 Cf. Richard Oliver, *Bertram Grosvenor Goodhue* (New York: Architectural History Foundation, 1983).

55 Shand-Tucci, p. 397.

56 Ralph Adams Cram, *Walled Towns* (Boston: Marshall Jones, 1919) and *The Ministry of Art* (Boston: Houghton Mifflin, 1914).

57 Shand-Tucci, pp. 148ff.

58 The notion of the *unheimlich* has been brought into the architectural debate by the architectural historian Anthony Vidler through a series of essays that culminated with his book *The Architectural Uncanny: Essays in the Modern Unhomely* (Cambridge, Mass.: MIT Press, 1992).

59 Robert Twombly, *Louis Sullivan: His Life and Work* (New York: Viking Books, 1986), pp. 52ff.

60 Vincent Scully, *American Architecture and Urbanism* (New York: Praeger, 1969), p. 108.

61 This sensibility pervades Sullivan's writing. See especially his "What Is Architecture?" in *Kindergarten Chats and Other Writings* (New York: Dover, 1979 [1918]), pp. 227–41.

62 *Kindergarten Chats*, p. 29.

63 Frank Lloyd Wright, "Designing Unity Temple," in *Writings and Buildings* (New York: New American Library, 1960 [1932]), pp. 74–83.

64 Cf. David G. DeLong, *Bruce Goff: Toward Absolute Architecture* (New York: Architectural History Foundation, 1988).

65 Ibid., p. 146.

66 Ibid., p. 122.

Chapter 3 *Queering Modernism*

1 Jane S. Smith, *Elsie de Wolfe: A Life in the High Style* (New York: Atheneum, 1982), p. 63.

2 Ibid., p. 64.

3 Ibid., p. 123.

4 Ibid., p. 141.

5 Sara Holmes Boutelle, *Julia Morgan, Architect* (New York: Abbeville Press, 1988), p. 154.

6 For a complete summary of Johnson's Life, see Franz Schulze, *Philip Johnson: Life and Works* (New York: Alfred A. Knopf, 1994).

7 Cf. Marc Treib, ed., *An Everyday Modernism: The Houses of William Wurster* (Berkeley, Calif.: University of California Press, 1995).

8 David Littlejohn, *Architect: The Life and Work of Charles W. Moore* (New York: Holt, Rinehart & Winston, 1984), pp. 13–14.

9 bid., p. 190.

10 Charles Moore, Gerald Allen, and Donlyn Lyndon, *The Place of Houses* (New York: Holt, Rinehart & Winston, 1974), p. 82.

11 Ibid., p. 207.

12 Ibid., p. 237.

13 Ibid., p. 121. Moore's last book was on the subject: *Water and Architecture* (New York: Harry N. Abrams, 1994).

14 Charles W. Moore, "The Yin, the Yang, and the Three Bears," in Eugene J. Johnson, ed., *Charles Moore: Buildings and Projects 1949–1986* (New York: Rizzoli International Publications, 1986), pp. 15–20, p. 15.

15 Robert Venturi, *Complexity and Contradiction in Architecture* (New York: Museum of Modern Art, 1966), p. 22.

16 Ibid., p. 103.

17 Ibid., p. 102.

Chapter 4 *From Cruising to Community*

1 The space of cruising is most ardently documented in the magazine *Steam: A Quarterly Journal for Men*, which records where one might find the best rest stops in Pennsylvania, the best cruising grounds at Los Angeles International Airport, or the best sex in the alleys of Bellingham, Washington. *Steam* even ventures into theory with such articles as John Paul Ricco's "Jacking Off: A Minor Architecture," *Steam*, Vol. 1, No. 4 (Winter 1994), pp. 236–42.

2 Marcel Proust, *In Search of Lost Time*, Vol. 4, *Sodom and Gomorrah*, trans. C. K. Scott Moncrieff and Terence Kilmartin (New York: Modern Library, 1993), pp. 23–25.

3 In the eighteenth century, there was even a rumored society seeking to create a queer utopia. See Margaret C. Jacob, "The Materialist World of Pornography," in Lynn Hunt, ed., *The Invention of Pornography: Obscenity and the Origins of Modernity, 1500–1800* (New York: Zone Books, 1993), pp. 157–202, p. 194.

4 Cf. Bruce Chatwin, *The Songlines* (New York: Viking Books, 1987).

5 John Rechy, *City of Night* (New York: Grove Weidenfeld, 1988 [1963], p. 9.

6 Ibid., p. 280.

7 John Rechy, *The Sexual Outlaw: A Documentary* (New York: Grove Weidenfeld, 1977), pp. 24–27.

8 Charles Bergengren, "Untitled: Opus 7 (This Is Folklore) *or* Purity and Danger: An Interpretation," in *New York Folklore*, Vol. 19, Nos. 1–2 (1993), pp. 121–54, pp. 145–48.

9 There is by now a substantial body of research on such spaces. See, for instance, Edward William Delph, *The Silent Community: Public Homosexual Encounters* (Beverly Hills, Calif.: Sage Publications, 1978), or David Woodhead, "'Surveillant Gays': HIV, Space and the Constitution of Identities," in David Bell and Gill Valentine, eds., *Mapping Desire: Geographies of Sexualities* (London: Routledge, 1995), pp. 231–44. The first study of this phenomenon, however, is Laud Humphreys, *Tearoom Trade: Impersonal Sex in Public Spaces* (Chicago: Aldine, 1970). For a perhaps more evocative text, see John Greyson, *Urinal and Other Stories* (Toronto: Art Metropole and the Power Plant, 1993).

10 Delph, p. 10.

11 For a good example of this, see George S. Snyder, "North East, Pennsylvania," in John Preston, ed., *Gay Men Write About Hometowns Where They Belong* (New York: Plume Books, 1992), pp. 97–109.

12 Paul Hallam, *The Book of Sodom* (London: Verso Press, 1993).

13 The best description of this futile effort comes in Richard Rodriguez's *Days of Obligation: An Argument with My Mexican Father* (New York: Penguin Books, 1992), p. 39.

14 For the conflation of the gym as a cruising ground and the faintly queer atmosphere of the men's club, see Alan Hollinghurst, *The Swimming Pool Library* (London: Chatto & Windus, 1988). There is also a substantial trade in illegal videotapes taken inside locker rooms.

15 Cf. Steven Maynard, "Through a Hole in the Lavatory Wall: Homosexual Subculture, Police Surveillance, and the Dialectics of Discovery," in *Journal of the History of Sexuality*, Vol. 5, No. 2 (October 1994), pp. 207–42.

16 George Chauncey, *Gay New York: Gender, Urban Culture, and the Making of the Gay Male World, 1890–1940* (New York: Basic Books, 1994).

17 Ibid., p. 168.

18 Cf. Barbara A. Weightman, "Bars as Private Places," *Landscape*, Vol. 24, No. 1 (1980), pp. 9–16.

19 There is not much documentation on this design, and many of the designers have died. I am indebted to David Dunlap for information on this issue, and for a copy of *Star Dust: News from The Saint*, Vol. 2, No. 2 (November 1982).

20 Edmund White, *States of Desire: Travels in Gay America* (New York: Plume Books, 1991 [1980], p. 267.

21 Chauncey, pp. 207–25.

22 Perhaps the best description of a bathhouse was, perhaps ironically, written by a straight woman: Rita Mae Brown, "Queen for a Day: A Stranger in Paradise," in Karla Jay and Allen Young, eds., *Lavender Culture* (New York: New York University Press, 1978), pp. 69–76.

23 Rodriguez, p. 44.

24 Henry Urbach, "Spatial Rubbing: The Zone," *Sites*, No. 25 (1993), pp. 90–95, p. 94.

25 Ibid.

26 Ibid., p. 95.

27 There have, by now, been numerous studies of this phenomenon in addition to the ones mentioned below. For early work, see Evelyn Hooker, "Male Homosexuals and Their Worlds," in Judd Marmor, ed., *Sexual Inversion: The Multiple Roots of Homosexuality* (New York: Basic Books, 1965), pp. 83–107; Mickey Lauria and Lawrence Knopp, "Toward an Analysis of the Role of Gay Communities in the Urban Renaissance," *Urban Geography*, Vol. 6 (April–June 1985), pp. 152–169; Martin P. Levine, "Gay Ghetto," in Martin P. Levine, ed., *The Sociology of Male Homosexuality* (New York: Harper & Row, 1979), pp. 182–204.

28 Martin P. Levine, "The Life and Death of Gay Clones," in Gilbert Herdt, ed., *Gay Culture in America: Essays from the Field* (Boston: Beacon Press, 1992), pp. 68–86, p. 76.

29 Frances FitzGerald, "The Castro," in *Cities on a Hill: A Journey Through Contemporary American Cultures* (New York: Simon & Schuster, 1981), pp. 25–119, p. 33.

30 Rodriguez, p. 29.

31 Manuel Castells, "Cultural Identity, Sexual Liberation and Urban Structure: The Gay Community in San Francisco," in *The City and the Grassroots: A Cross-Cultural Theory of Urban Social Movements* (Berkeley, Calif.: University of California Press, 1983), pp. 138–70, pp. 161–66.

32 Ibid., p. 157.

33 Michael Lassell, "Brooklyn/Long Island/Los Angeles/New York," in Preston, ed., p. 171.

34 Castells, p. 140.

35 Sy Adler and Johanna Brenner, "Gender and Space: Lesbians and Gay Men in the City," *International Journal of Urban and Regional Research*, No. 161 (1992), pp. 24–34.

36 Tamar Rothenberg, " 'And She Told Two Friends': Lesbians Creating Urban Social Space," in Bell and Valentine, eds., pp. 165–81.

37 Ibid., p. 180.

38 Daniel Mendelsohn, "The World Is a Ghetto," *OUT Magazine,* March 1995, pp. 79–83, 110–12. For the normalization of queer lives, see also "It's Normal to Be Queer," *The Economist,* January 6, 1996, pp.68–71

39 FitzGerald, p. 56.

Chapter 5 *The Void and Other Queer Spaces*

1 J. Huizinga, *Hertstij der Middeleeuwen: Studie over Levens-en Gedachtenvorming der Veertiende and Vijftiende Eeuw in Frankrijk and de Nederlanden* (Groningen: H. D. Tjeenk Willink, 1975 [1919]), esp. pp. 1–24.

2 "By [1983], the gay community of San Francisco had become for him a kind of magical 'heterotopia,' a place of dumbfounding excess that left him happily speechless. Promising a welcome 'limbo of nonidentity,' the city's countless bathhouses enabled Foucault as never before to grapple with his lifelong fascination with 'the overwhelming, the unspeakable, the creepy, the stupefying, the ecstatic,' embracing 'a pure violence, a wordless gesture'. . . This sentiment—that pleasure, for him, was somehow 'related to death'—had haunted Foucault throughout his life. . . . " James Miller, *The Passion of Michel Foucault* (New York: Anchor Books, 1993), pp. 26–27.

3 Richard Rodriguez, *Days of Obligation: An Argument with my Mexican Father* (New York: Penguin Books, 1993 [1992]), p. 30. In a similar vein, the city's architect Frank Israel noted about the relationship between his work and AIDS: "It opens me up to experience. These days I like going to Hollywood, where they're building the subway tunnel, and buying a taco at one of the stands. I eat it there, looking at the whole surreal scene: the white smoke, the hundreds of workers, the big hole in the ground. I take in the vision and I think it is very beautiful—not in the classical sense, but because it is something that is evolving, just as buildings are never resolved, just like my body is evolving. Someday something may come along to stop what's happening to me, but for now I am just changing." Interview with the author, December 7, 1994. Israel died of AIDS-related illnesses on June 9, 1996.

4 Ibid., p. 32.

5 Ibid., p. 33.

6 Ibid., p. 40.

7 David Wojnarowicz, *Close to the Knives: A Memoir of Disintegration* (New York: Vintage Books, 1991), p. 157.

8 Ibid., p. 17.

9 Ibid., p. 146.

10 Ibid., p. 109.

11 Matthew Stadler, *Landscape: Memory. A Novel* (New York: Charles Scribner's Sons, 1990); *The Dissolution of Nicholas Dee* (New York: Charles Scribner's Sons, 1993); *The Sex Offender* (New York: HarperCollins, 1994).

12 Alan Hollinghurst, *The Folding Star* (New York: Pantheon, 1994), p. 216.

13 Derek Jarman, *Chroma* (London: Vintage Books, 1995), p. 115.

14 Michel Foucault, "Other Spaces: The Principles of Heterotopia," *Lotus* 48–49 (1986), pp. 10–24.

15 Ibid., p. 12.

16 Ibid., p. 17.

Selected Bibliography

Adler, Sy, and Johanna Brenner. "Gender and Space: Lesbians and Gay Men in the City." *International Journal of Urban and Regional Research*, No. 161 (1992), pp. 24–34.

Alpers, Svetlana. "Seeing as Knowing: A Dutch Connection." *Humanities in Society* I (1978), pp. 147–73.

Arthur, Marilyn B. "The Dream of a World Without Women: Poetics and the Circles of Order in the *Theogony* Prooemium." *Arethusa,* Vol. 16, Nos. 1,2 (1983) pp. 97–116.

Beckford, William. *Vathek.* New York: Oxford University Press, 1983 (1786).

Bell, Arthur, Jim Fouratt, Kate Millet, Vito Russo, Jeff Weinstein, Edmund White, and Bertha Harris. "Extended Sensibilities: The Impact of Homosexual Sensibilities on Contemporary Culture." In Russell Ferguson, William Olander, Marcia Tucker, and Karen Fiss, eds., *Discourses: Conversations in Postmodern Art and Culture*, pp. 130–53. New York: New Museum of Contemporary Art, 1990.

Bell, David, and Gill Valentine, eds. *Mapping Desire: Geographies of Sexualities.* London: Routledge, 1995.

Benjamin, Walter. "Paris, Capital of the Nineteenth Century." In *Reflections: Essays, Aphorisms, Autobiographical Writings*, pp. 146–62. Trans. Edmund Jephcott. New York: Schocken Books, 1978.

Bergengren, Charles. "Untitled: Opus 7 (This Is Folklore) *or* Purity and Danger: An Interpretation." *New York Folklore*, Vol. 19, Nos. 1–2 (1993), pp. 121–154.

Bersani, Leo. *Homos.* Cambridge, Mass.: Harvard University Press, 1995.

Betsky, Aaron. *Building Sex: Men, Women, Architecture, and the Construction of Sexuality.* New York: William Morrow, 1995.

Boorstein, Jonathan. "Toward Identifying a Gay or Lesbian Aesthetic in Interior Design." Unpublished manuscript, 1984.

Boswell, John. *Christianity, Social Tolerance and Homosexuality: Gay People in Western Europe from the Beginning of the Christian Era to the Fourteenth Century.* Chicago: University of Chicago Press, 1980.

Boswell, John. *Same Sex Unions in Pre-Modern Europe.* New York: Random House, 1994.

Boutelle, Sara Holmes. *Julia Morgan, Architect.* New York: Abbeville Press, 1988.

Bronski, Michael. *Culture Clash: The Making of Gay Sensibility.* Boston: South End Press, 1984.

Bynum, Catherine Walker. *Fragmentation and Redemption: Essays on Gender and the Human Body in Medieval Religion.* New York: Zone Books, 1991.

Calloway, Stephen. " 'The Dandyism of the Senses': Aesthetic Ideals and Decadent Attitudes in the 1890s." In Michael Spense, ed., *The Studio: High Art and Low Life: "The Studio" and the Fin-de-Siècle* pp. 55–63. London: Victoria and Albert Museum, 1993.

Castells, Manuel. "Cultural Identity, Sexual Liberation and Urban Structure: The Gay Community in San Francisco." In *The City and the Grassroots: A Cross-Cultural Theory of Urban Social Movements*, pp. 138–70. Berkeley, Calif.: University of California Press, 1983.

Chauncey, George. *Gay New York: Gender, Urban Culture, and the Making of the Gay Male World, 1890–1940.* New York: Basic Books, 1994.

Clark, T. J. *The Painting of Modern Life: Paris in the Art of Manet and His Followers.* New York: Alfred A. Knopf, 1985.

Cram, Ralph Adams. *Walled Towns.* Boston: Marshall Jones, 1919.

Crawford, Alan. *C. R. Ashbee: Architect, Designer and Romantic Socialist.* New Haven, Conn.: Yale University Press, 1985.

Creed, Gerald W. "Sexual Subordination: Institutionalized Homosexuality and Social Control in Melanesia." In Jonathan Goldberg, ed. *Reclaiming Sodom*, pp. 66–94. New York: Routledge, 1994.

DeLong, David G. *Bruce Goff: Toward Absolute Architecture.* New York: Architectural History Foundation, 1988.

Delph, Edward William. *The Silent Community: Public Homosexual Encounters.* Beverly Hills, Calif.: Sage Publications, 1978.

De Sade, Marquis. *The 120 Days of Sodom and Other Writing.* Trans. Austryn Wainhouse and Richard Seaver. New York: Grove Weidenfeld, 1966.

Dollimore, Jonathan. *Sexual Dissidence: Augustine to Wilde, Freud to Foucault.* Oxford, England: Clarendon Press, 1993.

Dowling, Elizabeth Meredith. *American Classicist: The Architecture of Philip Trammell Shutze.* New York: Rizzoli Publications, 1989.

Fernandez, Dominique. "Kitsch Rex." *Connaissance des Arts*, Vol. 5, Nos. 413/414 (July/August 1988), pp. 18–27.

FitzGerald, Frances. "The Castro." In *Cities on a Hill: A Journey Through Contemporary American Cultures*, pp. 25–119. New York: Simon & Schuster, 1981.

Foucault, Michel. *The History of Sexuality.* Trans. Robert Hurley. New York: Vintage Books, 1978.

Foucault, Michel. "Other Spaces: The Principles of Heterotopia." *Lotus* 48/49 (1986), pp. 10–24.

Genet, Jean. *The Miracle of the Rose.* In The *Selected Writings of Jean Genet,* pp. 50–108. Trans. Bernard Frechtman. Hopewell, N.J.: Ecco Press, 1993 (1949).

Gleanzer, Richard Butler, ed. *Decorative Art in America: A Lecture by Oscar Wilde, Together with Letters, Reviews and Interviews.* New York: Brentano's, 1906.

Goldberg, Jonathan, ed. *Queering the Renaissance.* Durham, N.C.: Duke University Press, 1994.

Graham, Kenneth W., ed. *Vathek and the Escape from Time: Bicentenary Revaluations.* New York: AMS Press, 1990.

Greenberg, David F. *The Construction of Homosexuality.* Chicago: University of Chicago Press, 1988.

Greyson, John. *Urinal and Other Stories.* Toronto: Art Metropole and the Power Plant, 1993.

Hallam, Paul. *The Book of Sodom.* London: Verso Press, 1993.

Halsall, Paul. "The Experience of Homosexuality in the Middle Ages." Unpublished manuscript posted on the World Wide Web.

Herdt, Gilbert H. *Guardians of the Flutes: Idioms of Masculinity.* New York: McGraw-Hill, 1981.

Herdt, Gilbert H., ed. *Gay Culture in America: Essays from the Field.* Boston: Beacon Press, 1992.

Holland, Vyvyan. *Son of Oscar Wilde.* New York: E. P. Dutton, 1954.

Hollinghurst, Alan. *The Folding Star.* New York: Pantheon, 1994.

Hollinghurst, Alan. *The Swimming Pool Library.* London: Chatto & Windus, 1988.

Hooker, Evelyn. "Male Homosexuals and Their Worlds." In Judd Marmor, ed., *Sexual Inversion: The Multiple Roots of Homosexuality,* pp. 83–107. New York: Basic Books, 1965.

Humphreys, Laud. *Tearoom Trade: Impersonal Sex in Public Spaces.* Chicago: Aldine, 1970.

Hunt, Lynn, ed. *The Invention of Pornography: Obscenity and the Origins of Modernity, 1500–1800.* New York: Zone Books, 1993.

Huysmans, Joris-Karl. *Against Nature.* Trans. Robert Baldick. New York: Penguin Books, 1959 (1884).

Jarman, Derek. *Chroma.* London: Vintage Books, 1995.

Jay, Karla, and Allen Young, eds. *Lavender Culture.* New York: New York University Press, 1978.

Jervis, Simon. "Ludwig II of Bavaria: His Architecture, Design and Decoration in Context." In Roy Strong and Lisa Taylor, eds., *Designs for the Dream King: The Castles and Palaces of Ludwig II of Bavaria,* pp. 9–21. London: Debrett's Peerage Ltd., 1978.

Johnson, Eugene J., ed. *Charles Moore: Buildings and Projects 1949–1986.* New York: Rizzoli International Publications, 1986.

Keuls, Eva C. *The Reign of the Phallus: Sexual Politics in Ancient Athens.* New York: Harper & Row, 1985.

Lacan, Jacques. *Écrits: A Selection*. Trans. Alan Sheridan. New York: W. W. Norton, 1977.

Lauria, Mickey, and Lawrence Knopp. "Toward an Analysis of the Role of Gay Communities in the Urban Renaissance." *Urban Geography,* Vol. 6 (April–June 1985), pp. 152–69.

Lears, T. J. Jackson. "Infinite Riches in a Little Room: The Interior Scenes of Modernist Culture." *Modulus* 18 (1987), pp. 3–27.

Lears, T. J. Jackson. *No Place of Grace: Antimodernism and the Transformation of American Culture, 1880–1920*. New York: Pantheon, Books, 1981.

Lees-Milne, James. *William Beckford*. London: Compton Russell, 1976.

Levine, Martin P., ed. *The Sociology of Male Homosexuality*. New York: Harper & Row, 1979.

Littlejohn, David. *Architect: The Life and Work of Charles W. Moore*. New York: Holt, Rinehart and Winston, 1984.

Maynard, Steven. "Through a Hole in the Lavatory Wall: Homosexual Subculture, Police Surveillance, and the Dialectics of Discovery." *Journal of the History of Sexuality,* Vol. 5, No. 2 (October 1994), pp. 207–42.

Meer, Theo van der. "Sodomy and the Pursuit of a Third Sex in the Early Modern Period." In Gilbert Herdt, ed., *Third Sex, Third Gender: Beyond Sexual Dimorphism in Culture and History*, pp. 137–212. New York: Zone Books, 1994.

Meyer, Moe. *The Politics and Poetics of Camp*. London: Routledge, 1994.

Miller, James. *The Passion of Michel Foucault*. New York: Anchor Books, 1993.

Moore, Charles, Gerald Allen, and Donlyn Lyndon. *The Place of Houses*. New York: Holt, Rinehart & Winston, 1974.

Newton, Esther. *Cherry Grove, Fire Island: Sixty Years in America's First Gay and Lesbian Town*. New York: Beacon Books, 1993.

Oliver, Richard. *Bertram Grosvenor Goodhue*. New York: Architectural History Foundation, 1983.

Ortner, Sherry B., and Harriet Whitehead, eds. *Sexual Meanings: The Cultural Construction of Gender and Sexuality.* Cambridge, England: Cambridge University Press, 1981.

Praz, Mario. *An Illustrated History of Interior Decoration from Pompeii to Art Nouveau.* London: Thames & Hudson, 1981 (1964).

Preston, John, ed. *Gay Men Write About Hometowns Where They Belong.* New York: Plume Books, 1992.

Proust, Marcel. *In Search of Lost Time.* Vol. 4, *Sodom and Gomorrah.* Trans. C. K. Scott Moncrieff and Terence Kilmartin. New York: Modern Library, 1993.

Rechy, John. *City of Night.* New York: Grove Weidenfeld, 1988 (1963).

Rechy, John. *The Sexual Outlaw: A Documentary.* New York: Grove Weidenfeld, 1977.

Ricco, John Paul. "Jacking Off: A Minor Architecture." *Steam,* Vol. 1, No. 4 (Winter 1994), pp. 236–42.

Rodriguez, Richard. *Days of Obligation: An Argument with My Mexican Father.* New York: Penguin Books, 1992.

Schulze, Franz. *Philip Johnson: Life and Works.* New York: Alfred A. Knopf, 1994.

Sedgwick, Eve Kosofsky. *Epistemology of the Closet.* Berkeley, Calif.: University of California Press, 1990.

Sennett, Richard. *Flesh and Stone: The Body and the City in Western Civilization.* New York: W. W. Norton, 1994.

Shand-Tucci, Douglass. *Boston Bohemia 1881–1900.* Vol. 1 of *Ralph Adams Cram: Life and Architecture.* Amherst, Mass.: University of Massachusetts Press, 1995.

Sinfield, Alan. *The Wilde Century: Effeminacy, Oscar Wilde and the Queer Movement.* London: Cassell, 1994.

Smith, Jane S. *Elsie de Wolfe: A Life in the High Style.* New York: Atheneum, 1982.

Spain, Daphne. *Gendered Spaces.* Chapel Hill, N.C.: University of North Carolina Press, 1992.

Sontag, Susan. "Notes on Camp." In *A Susan Sontag Reader,* pp. 105–19. New York: Farrar, Straus & Giroux, 1982 (1964).

Twombly, Robert. *Louis Sullivan: His Life and Work.* New York: Viking Books, 1986.

Urbach, Henry. "Spatial Rubbing: The Zone." *Sites*, No. 25 (1993), pp. 90–95.

Venturi, Robert. *Complexity and Contradiction in Architecture.* New York: Museum of Modern Art, 1966.

Vidler, Anthony. *The Architectural Uncanny: Essays in the Modern Unhomely.* Cambridge, Mass.: MIT Press, 1992.

Weeks, Jeffrey. *Sexuality and Its Discontents: Meanings, Myths and Modern Sexualities.* London: Routledge & Kegan Paul, 1985.

Weightman, Barbara A. "Bars as Private Places." *Landscape,* Vol. 24, No. 1 (1980), pp. 9–16.

White, Edmund. *States of Desire: Travels in Gay America.* New York: Plume Books, 1991 (1980).

Whittle, Stephen, ed. *The Margins of the City: Gay Men's Urban Lives.* London: Ashgate Publishing, 1994.

Wojnarowicz, David. *Close to the Knives: A Memoir of Disintegration.* New York 1991: Vintage Books.

Yegül, Fikret. *Baths and Bathing in Classical Antiquity.* New York: Architectural History Foundation, 1992.

Illustration Credits

Introduction I.1, Robin Platzer
I.2, Museum of the City of New York,
The Byron Collection

Chapter 1 1.2, courtesy of Deutsches Institut
für Filmkunde, Frankfurt am Main,
Germany
1.5, © Musée de l'Homme, Paris;
Photo Van den Broek
1.8, courtesy of the Board of Trustees
of the National Museums
and Galleries on Merseyside
(Walker Art Gallery, Liverpool)
1.13, photograph by Shirley Burden
1.15, © Steve Jaycox

Chapter 2 2.12, courtesy of the Victoria and
Albert Museum, London
2.14, courtesy of the Victoria and
Albert Museum, London
2.20, courtesy of the Chicago
Historical Society

Chapter 3 3.1a, courtesy of the Museum
of the City of New York,
The Byron Collection
3.1b, courtesy of the Museum
of the City of New York,
The Byron Collection
3.3, photograph by Richard Barnes
3.8a, courtesy of the Cecil Beaton
Archives, Sotheby's, London

Chapter 3 3.8b, photograph by Derry Moore
3.9, courtesy of the Cecil Beaton
Archives, Sotheby's, London
3.10, photograph by
Richard Payne, FAIA
3.12, photograph by
Richard Payne, FAIA
3.13, photograph by
Richard Payne, FAIA
3.14, photograph by
Morley Baer
3.15, photograph by
Morley Baer
3.16b, photograph by
Morley Baer
3.18, photograph by
Morley Baer
3.20, courtesy of Venturi
and Scott Brown, Architects
3.21, courtesy of Venturi
and Scott Brown, Architects
3.22, courtesy of Venturi
and Scott Brown, Architects
3.23, photograph by Ed Stoecklein;
courtesy of Robert A. M. Stern,
Architects
3.24, photograph by
Timothy Hursley;
3.25, photograph by
Timothy Hursley

Chapter 4 4.1, photograph © 1996,
The Art Institute of Chicago,
all rights reserved; gift of
Georgia O'Keefe, 1949
4.2a, Lesbian and Gay Community
Services Center, National Archive
of Lesbian and Gay History
4.2b, Lesbian and Gay Community
Services Center, National Archive
of Lesbian and Gay History
4.4, photograph by Jim Grimes 4.6,
Lesbian and Gay Community Services
Center, National Archive of Lesbian
and Gay History
4.7, © Steve Jaycox
4.8, courtesy of the Fogg Art Museum
4.9, © Steve Jaycox
4.11, photograph by Jim Grimes

Chapter 5 5.2a, courtesy of Mark Robbins
5.2b, photograph by Grant Taylor;
courtesy of Mark Robbins
5.3, courtesy of Durham Crout
5.4a, © 1994 by the Estate
of David Wojnarowicz
5.4b, © 1994 by the Estate
of David Wojnarowicz
5.5, courtesy of Musée du Louvre

Index

Page numbers in italics refer to captions.